MERE
CATHOLICISM

MERE
CATHOLICISM

*What the Catholic Church
teaches and practices*

John F. Fink

To order additional copies of this book, contact:
Xlibris LLC
1-888-795-4274
www.Xlibris.com
Orders@Xlibris.com
139298

TABLE OF CONTENTS

Also by John F. Fink:

Moments in Catholic History

Travels With Jesus in the Holy Land

Married Saints

The Doctors of the Church:
Doctors of the First Millennium

The Doctors of the Church:
Doctors of the Second Millennium

American Saints

Future American Saints?

Letters to St. Francis de Sales: Mostly on Prayer

Jesus in the Gospels

Biblical Women

Saint Thomas More: Model for Modern Catholics

Patriotic Leaders of the Church

Memoirs of a Catholic Journalist

The Mission and Future of the Catholic Press
(Editor)

PREFACE

Yes, of course the title for this book came from C. S. Lewis's book *Mere Christianity*, his masterpiece of Christian apologetics. Whereas he wrote about Christianity in general, carefully refraining from teaching the doctrine of any particular denomination, this book is meant to explain specifically what Catholics believe and practice. He avoided any topics that would take him, as he said, "into highly controversial regions," and the example he gave was "more about the Blessed Virgin Mary than is involved in asserting the Virgin Birth of Christ." Catholicism, of course, doesn't avoid those controversial issues, and so neither does this book.

On the other hand, I thought it permissible to use the word "mere" in relation to Catholicism. Anybody who knows a number of Catholics will realize that not all of them agree about everything. There are conservative or traditional Catholics and there are liberal or progressive Catholics. Some Catholics are Democrats and some are Republicans. Some Catholics go to Mass daily and pray frequently throughout the day, and others are less devout. In other words, there is a legitimate pluralism in the Catholic Church.

However, there are also basic doctrines that all Catholics are required to believe and there are basic devotions that all Catholics are expected to practice. Most of those doctrines—but not all—are included in the Catholic Church's two creeds, the Nicene Creed and the Apostles' Creed. Anyone who doesn't accept those doctrines should not go around calling himself or herself a Catholic.

Just as C. S. Lewis's book *Mere Christianity* was meant to be non-controversial for all Christians, so this book is meant to be non-controversial for all Catholics. It includes many doctrines and devotions that Lewis didn't touch on because those are doctrines and devotions that the Catholic Church teaches and practices. They might be controversial among different Christian denominations, but they shouldn't be controversial for Catholics.

This book, then, is about the basic teachings and practices of the Catholic Church. It is meant both for Catholics, to give them a better understanding of what their Church teaches and practices, and for people who might be attracted to the Catholic Church, perhaps precisely because of its doctrines and devotions. However, it is not a catechism. Thankfully, the Catholic Church now has excellent catechisms, including the *Catechism of the Catholic Church* and the *United States Catholic Catechism for Adults*, both of which I quote frequently—and consulted even more frequently if I didn't actually quote from them. Both of those catechisms, though, are lengthy and I thought Catholics, and those considering Catholicism, should have something a bit more manageable. I hope the length of this book is about right.

This book, too, is meant to be a popular rather than a scholarly book. Therefore, I've dispensed with footnotes, although I have noted biblical references and quotations from the catechisms in the text.

C. S. Lewis's *Mere Christianity* began as talks given over the radio in England in the early 1940s and were then published in three separate parts before being brought together in one book. Many of the chapters in this book began as columns in periodicals, especially *The Criterion*, the newspaper for the Catholic Archdiocese of Indianapolis. I have been writing a weekly column and editorials for *The Criterion* since I became its editor in 1984 (I'm now its editor emeritus), so many of the ideas in this book first saw the light of day there. It worked the other direction, too. Many of my columns in *The Criterion* during the Catholic Church's "Year of Faith," from October 11, 2012 through November 24, 2013, have been condensations of chapters in this book. A few chapters also began as talks that I gave about Catholicism.

I would like to express my appreciation to those at Xlibris who helped bring this book to completion.

CHAPTER 1

"WE BELIEVE IN ONE GOD"

It should be obvious that Catholics believe in God. In this, of course, we are hardly a minority, at least in the United States, because polls show consistently that more than nine out of ten Americans share that belief. In fact, a 2008 study by the Pew Forum on Religion & Public Life revealed that only 1.6 percent of Americans are atheists and only 2.4 percent call themselves agnostics.

Belief in God is also shared by most of the people in the history of the world—the ancient Egyptians, Greeks, Romans, Orientals, Arabs, savages in the New World discovered by Columbus, and those in Indonesia. Although atheism is making inroads in Western Europe, most people in the rest of the world believe in God. We believe that, as the *Catechism of the Catholic Church* says, "The desire for God is written in the human heart, because man is created by God and for God" (No. 27).

Unlike the ancients, though, Catholics join with Jews, Muslims, and other Christians, to profess belief in *one* God. Our Creed, which we recite at Mass on Sundays, begins, "We believe in one God." In this we differ from the Hindus, for example, who worship many gods. We believe in only one God because God himself has revealed himself to us that he is only one. Therefore, what Catholics believe about God comes from both reason and revelation.

Can we prove that God exists? Not in a way that modern science would accept because no one can produce God and say, "There he is." But theologians have produced convincing arguments for his existence. Saint Thomas Aquinas in the thirteenth century offered five proofs, but they're a bit technical and I will bypass summarizing them. For most people, though, the order, harmony and beauty of the world are reason enough to believe in an intelligent Creator.

We believe that God always was and always will be; he had no beginning and will have no end. He is almighty, omnipotent, meaning that he can do everything that isn't contradictory (like making a square circle). He is omniscient, all-knowing. He is perfect goodness and, as Saint John's Gospel tells us, he is love. Saint Anselm defined God in his *Prologion* as "a being than whom nothing greater can be conceived." And God himself revealed himself to Moses in the Bible's Book of Exodus as "I am who am."

The First Vatican Council, which met in 1869 and 1870, said that God is "the one, true, living God, Creator and Lord of heaven and earth, omnipotent, eternal, immense, incomprehensible, infinite in intellect and will and in every perfection . . . one unique spiritual substance, wholly simple and unchanging . . . really and essentially distinct from the world, totally blessed in himself and of himself and ineffably elevated above all things which are and can be thought of apart from him." That's what Catholics believe about God.

Some people might say, "OK, I believe that God exists and even that he created the world, but then he left us all to our own devices." These people are called Deists and many of the Founding Fathers of this country believed in Deism. Catholics do not. We believe in a personal God who loves each one of us and wants what is best for us. That's why we can, and must, pray to God with prayers of adoration, praise, petition, thanksgiving, intercession, and contrition. Catholics, along with most other Christians, believe strongly in the power of prayer.

For some people, the evil that exists in the world is a large stumbling block to their belief in a good God. "How could God permit evil to exist if he is all-good?" they will ask. Catholicism's answer is that God freely chose to create a world that is not perfect but which is on a journey toward perfection. This is true for both physical evils, such as hurricanes or tornadoes, and moral evil, such as sin. As regards moral evil, God chose to bestow on humans the gift of free will, enabling us to choose to commit sin. I'll discuss this in more detail in Chapter 5, but thought I should mention it here, too.

CHAPTER 2

GOD AS CREATOR

In our Creed, we Catholics say that we believe in one God, "the Father, the Almighty, maker of heaven and earth, of all that is, seen and unseen." We believe that God created the world. However, we do not reject scientific facts, as many people suppose we do.

In recent years, atheism has become our society's latest fad. It started with the success of British atheist Richard Dawkins' book *The God Delusion.* American atheist Sam Harris also had a best-seller, called *The End of Faith: Religion, Terror, and the Future of Reason.* He followed that up with *Letter to a Christian Nation*, which also achieved success. He argued, in effect, that religious beliefs are mainly responsible for most of the evil in the world.

These books argue that science and belief in God are incompatible. But Catholics insist that there cannot be incompatibility between science and religion because God is the author of both. It's true that Catholic Church officials were once wrong when they condemned the teachings of Galileo that the earth revolves about the sun, but the Church has learned from that mistake.

The Catholic Church teaches that God created the universe, but not the way the Book of Genesis described the creation. Since at least the time of Saint Augustine in the fifth century, the accounts of creation in Genesis have been seen as largely symbolic. The Bible is not a scientific textbook. If the congregation of cardinals that condemned Galileo in the seventeenth century had been more aware of that, the split between science and religion would not have occurred.

Some atheists who put all their faith in science want to give the impression that most scientists are atheists. That simply isn't true. As far as I know, there is no study that shows that there's a greater percentage of atheists among scientists than there is in other professions. Atheists remain a small minority among scientists just as they do in other fields. Throughout history, our greatest scientists have tended to be believers, many of them devout believers. Sometimes that belief comes from recognition that there is tremendous order in the universe, an order that could not have occurred accidentally.

Pope Emeritus Benedict spoke about Christianity and science on November 6, 2006 in a talk to the Pontifical Academy of the Sciences. Here are excerpts:

"Christianity does not posit an inevitable conflict between supernatural faith and scientific progress. The very starting-point of biblical revelation is the affirmation that God created human beings, endowed them with reason, and set them over all the creatures of the earth. In this way, man has become the steward of creation and God's 'helper.'" . . .

"Man cannot place in science and technology so radical and unconditional a trust as to believe that scientific and technological progress can explain everything and completely fulfill all his existential and spiritual needs. Science cannot replace philosophy and revelation by giving an exhaustive answer to man's most radical questions: questions about the meaning of living and dying; about ultimate values, and about the nature of progress itself."

Pope John Paul II, Pope Emeritus Benedict's predecessor, wrote in 1986, "The theory of natural evolution, understood in a sense that does not exclude divine causality, is not in principle opposed to the truth about the creation of the visible world, as presented in the Book of Genesis." He was even stronger in 1996, in a message to the Pontifical Academy of Sciences, when he said that "the theory of evolution has a great deal of scientific basis."

Back in 1925, when G. K. Chesterton wrote his masterpiece *The Everlasting Man* to refute some of the claims of H. G. Wells, he began with a discussion of evolution and its limitations. He noted, "It is really far more logical to start by saying 'In the beginning God created heaven and earth' even if you only mean 'In the beginning some unthinkable power began some unthinkable process.'"

Author Frank J. Sheed, in his book *Theology and Sanctity*, pointed out that Genesis "tells us of the fact but not the process: there was an assembling of elements of the material universe, but was it instantaneous or spread over a considerable space and time? Was it complete in one act, or by stages?"

The Catholic Church doesn't pretend to know the answer to that question.

CHAPTER 3

THE CENTRAL MYSTERY OF
THE CHRISTIAN FAITH

We have seen that most people in the world today, and most people in the history of the world, believe or believed in God. Christians are unique, though, in that we believe in the Holy Trinity. People can come to belief in God through reason, but knowledge of, and belief in, the Trinity must come from revelation, especially since it seems at first glance to be contradictory, saying that something is both three and one. Since this dogma is a mystery we cannot fully understand it.

The dogma of the Trinity is not only *a* mystery, it is *the* central mystery of Christian faith and life. The *Catechism of the Catholic Church* goes so far as to say, quoting Saint Caesarius of Arles, that "the faith of all Christians rests on the Trinity" (No. 232). We are baptized "in the name of the Father and of the Son and of the Holy Spirit"—the three persons in the Holy Trinity. We profess our faith in the Trinity every time we make the Sign of the Cross.

Since it is the central mystery of our faith—the most fundamental and essential teaching in the hierarchy of the truths of faith and the source of all the other mysteries of faith—we should not take it for granted. Doctrines that depend upon the proper understanding of the Trinity were the subject of the earliest church councils, and even today the Catholic and Orthodox Churches disagree over one aspect of the doctrine.

The dogma states that there is only one God but that he is three persons—Father, Son and Holy Spirit—sharing one divine nature. The three persons are co-equal, co-eternal, and consubstantial, that is, they share the same substance. When we make the Sign of the Cross, we do so in the "name" of the Father, Son and Holy Spirit, not the "names," because there is only one God.

Most Catholics undoubtedly accept the dogma of the Trinity without fully understanding the theology behind it. But for the record, the three persons in the Trinity are differentiated from one another by virtue of their relationships. Thus the Father begets the Son and then the Holy Spirit is spirated by, or proceeds from, the Father and the Son. This did not happen at some time in history but eternally. Otherwise there would have been a time when the Son and the Holy Spirit did not exist, and that's impossible since they are God.

This mystery was unknown throughout the time of the Old Testament. God revealed it to us in its fullness only after the Incarnation of his Son and with the sending of the Holy Spirit on Pentecost. The earliest Christian writings acknowledged this dogma and it soon became part of the Eucharistic liturgy.

The first ecumenical council at Nicaea in 325 taught that the Son of God, who became human, was "consubstantial" with the Father. The second council at Constantinople in 381 kept that expression when it formulated the Nicene Creed and said that Jesus Christ was "the only-begotten Son of God, eternally begotten of the Father, light from light, true God from true God, begotten not made, consubstantial with the Father."

That same council taught that the Holy Spirit is "the Lord and giver of life, who proceeds from the Father." Later the Western Church added that the Spirit "proceeds from the Father and the Son," and this is the source of disagreement with the Orthodox Churches. They insist that the Holy Spirit proceeds from the Father *through* the Son. The Catholic Church's wording emphasizes that all three persons are one substance while the Eastern tradition emphasizes that the three persons are separate and distinct. However, the Catholic Church also teaches that the divine persons are really distinct from one another but that this distinctiveness resides solely in their relationships to one another. The differences in the wording are considered so slight that it's generally agreed that the Catholic and Orthodox Churches could come to an agreement if they could solve the other matter that keeps them separated—mainly, the role of the pope.

CHAPTER 4

BELIEF IN ORIGINAL SIN

As Catholics, we believe that Jesus suffered and died for our salvation, and I'll discuss that in detail in later chapters. But first we must ask the question: why do we need salvation?

Because, Catholics believe, we were born with original sin on our souls. And what is original sin? It's the sin of Adam and Eve, described in the second and third chapters of the biblical Book of Genesis. The sin was personal to them but passed on to all persons as a state of privation of grace. Catholics believe that Adam's sin of disobedience has been transmitted to all humans, depriving us of the original holiness and justice in which Adam and Eve were created.

Adam and Eve? Does that mean that the Catholic Church takes the Book of Genesis literally, that there really was an Adam and Eve? Not exactly. It teaches that the Book of Genesis was an inspired religious book but not an inspired scientific book. It will allow scientists to determine, if they can, whether the human race emerged from a single primate population or from several geographically separated populations.

Whichever happened, Genesis teaches that the first humans sinned and thereby lost the original justice and holiness with which God endowed them. It uses figurative rather than literal language but describes an event that took place at the beginning of the history of the human race. Man and woman abused the freedom that God gave them, opposed God and separated themselves from him.

The late biblical expert Father Raymond Brown wrote that "we should recognize how well the ingenious biblical story of Adam and Eve conveyed the idea of sin and its origins and not think that we will find a better modern substitute for telling that story."

As a result of original sin, human nature is weakened in its powers. It is subject to ignorance, suffering and death. As a result of original sin, we humans are also inclined to commit sins, an inclination called "concupiscence."

And that is why the human race needed salvation. Only by understanding the nature of original sin can we understand the mystery of why God sent his Son to be our savior. I think the idea of original sin has been dismissed by a lot of people, but it's essential if the doctrine of Christ's dying for our salvation and redemption is to make sense.

It seems to me that there are a lot of Pelagianists in our modern world. Pelagianism was a fifth-century heresy that originated with an Irish monk named Pelagius. He taught, among other things, that men and women could, by the natural power of free will and without the necessary help of God's grace, lead a morally good life. He reduced Adam's fault basically to bad example.

Pelagius taught that Adam was made mortal and would have died whether he had sinned or not; that Adam's sin injured only him and not the human race; and that newborn children are in the same state as Adam before his fall. Saint Augustine, considered the greatest of all the Fathers of the Western Church, combated Pelagius's teachings and developed the doctrine of grace. He is called the Doctor of Grace.

According to Augustine and the Catholic Church, grace is a created sharing or participation in the life of God, given to persons through the merits of Christ and communicated by the Holy Spirit. It is a free gift of God and is necessary for salvation. Grace is received through the sacrament of baptism.

Baptism removes sins, not only original sin but also personal sins. It doesn't, however, restore us to the same state enjoyed by Adam before his fall. We still suffer illness, death and concupiscence. But it enables us to know, love and serve God through the theological virtues, and grow in goodness through the moral virtues. It is how we are "born again" and thus able to enjoy the salvation won for us by Christ.

CHAPTER 5

WHY EVIL EXISTS

As I noted briefly in Chapter 1, those who don't believe in God sometimes point to all the evil that exists in the world as the basis for their disbelief. If God is supposed to be all-good and all-powerful, they say, where was he during the Holocaust or the numerous natural calamities that take the lives of innocent people?

Put another way, if there is such an all-powerful and all-good God, why didn't he create a world so perfect that no evil could exist in it? Unfortunately, there is no quick answer. God could have created a better world, but he chose not to. Instead, in his infinite wisdom, he willed to create a world in a state of journeying toward an ultimate perfection. During that journey there exists both physical good and physical evil, including both constructive and destructive forces of nature.

In particular, God chose to carry out his plan for the world by making use of his creatures' cooperation. He gave us humans not only existence but the dignity of acting on our own. He had so much trust in us that he gave us free will. It's a gift he gave only to his highest creatures, to angels and humans.

By giving us free will, God has made it possible for us to go astray, and it was precisely by humans exercising a free choice that moral evil entered the world. This does not, however, make God responsible for moral evil. He permits it because he respects the freedom he gave his creatures.

Anyone in authority should understand how free will works. Perhaps a father tells his son, "You've got to learn to help around the house. I'm not going to insist on it, but I'd like you to rake up the leaves in the yard when you come home from school." When the father comes home from work he finds his son playing with his friends. The father wanted his son to rake the leaves but his son freely chose to do something else.

That's the way it works between God and humans: God wants us to do what is right but he has given us the power to decide for ourselves. We can freely choose to do something good and we can also freely choose to do something bad.

Of course, God knew in advance that humans would sometimes use their freedom to do evil. But he wanted his higher creatures to be able to freely unite themselves to him and to each other. An entire world of creatures that worked like machines couldn't freely give him praise. Why would he bother to create such a world? Of course, he didn't.

There is also this: God somehow knows how to derive good out of evil. Saint Augustine wrote that God, "because he is supremely good, would never allow any evil whatsoever to exist in his works if he were not so all-powerful and good as to cause good to emerge from evil itself."

It is often hard to figure out, in individual cases, how that could happen. Joseph in the Book of Genesis knew that he was the victim of evil when his brothers sold him into slavery in Egypt and he couldn't imagine good coming from that evil. Later, though, it was clear to him and he told his brothers, "You meant evil against me, but God meant it for good, to achieve his present end, the survival of many people" (Genesis 50:29).

For us Christians, the greatest moral evil ever committed was the murder of God's Son, an evil that brought the greatest good: Christ's glorification and our redemption.

CHAPTER 6

THE INCARNATION

"The Word was made flesh and dwelt among us" (John 1:14).

That's how John's Gospel reported the magnificent mystery of the Incarnation, the amazing fact that Almighty God actually lowered himself to become a human being. John tells us as plainly as possible, "In the beginning was the Word" (he existed from all eternity), "and the Word was with God, and *the Word was God*" (John 1:1). To make it even clearer, he identifies the Word with creation, saying, "All things came to be through him, and without him nothing came to be" (John 1:3).

Catholics profess their belief in the Incarnation when we recite the Creed during Mass on Sundays. We say that we believe in "one Lord, Jesus Christ, the only Son of God" who "was born of the Virgin Mary and became man."

Saint Paul also taught the preexistence of Jesus Christ. In his Letter to the Philippians, written perhaps as early as 55 A.D., he quoted a hymn that already existed: "Jesus Christ, who, though he was in the form of God, did not regard equality with God something to be grasped. Rather, he emptied himself, taking the form of a slave, coming in human likeness" (Philippians 2:6-7).

Paul wrote about God sending his Son in other letters, too. For example, to the Galatians he wrote, "When the fullness of time had fully come, God sent forth his Son, born of a woman" (Galatians 4:4). To the Romans he wrote, "Sending his own Son in the likeness of sinful flesh . . ." (Romans 8:3).

This has been the belief of Christians down through the centuries—that Jesus was true God, existing from all eternity and through whom all things were made, but at a particular moment in history also became a human being. He was both God and man, fully human with all our imperfections and weaknesses while remaining the perfect and infinitely powerful God. He is not part God and part man or some confused mixture but fully human while remaining God.

But can modern people believe that God really came down from heaven, became a fully human person, lived a dramatic life teaching the right way to live, died a horrible death as a criminal, rose from the dead and then went back to heaven? Isn't all this in the realm of myth?

That's what C. S. Lewis thought when he was a young lecturer at Oxford. Then, as he described in his book *Surprised by Joy*, one night he heard another committed atheist remark that the evidence for the historicity of the Gospels was surprisingly good. Lewis came to realize that myths are not false simply because they are myths. He later was so famously to write that "the heart of Christianity is a myth which is also a fact." His understanding that led to his conversion to Christianity.

But why did God choose to assume our human nature? Various reasons are given: The Word became flesh in order to save us by reconciling us with God; so that thus we might know God's love; to be our model of holiness; to make us partakers of the divine nature. The ultimate reason, though, is because God had to assume a human nature in order to accomplish our salvation, our redemption, in it. That couldn't be done by just any human but it did require a human to do it. Since Jesus is divine and human, he is the one and only mediator between God and humans.

Because we have been redeemed by the God-man, we humans can share God's divine nature. Ever since the beginning of Christian theology, the reason for the Incarnation has been "so that man, by entering into communion with the Word and thus receiving divine sonship, might become a son of God" (Irenaeus, second century).

Or as Saint Athanasius wrote in the fourth century, "God became man so that man might become God."

In the thirteenth century, Saint Thomas Aquinas said, "The only-begotten Son of God, wanting to make us sharers in his divinity, assumed our nature, so that he, made man, might make men gods."

CHAPTER 7

THE DIVINITY OF JESUS

For much of the twentieth century certain scholars attempted to find "the historical Jesus" as opposed, I suppose, to the Jesus of the Christian faith. While trying to learn as much as possible about the Jewish man whose followers came to believe was God-made-flesh, they sometimes acknowledge that he was a great man but deny that he was divine.

But it is not sufficient for Catholics to follow Christ just because he was a great man. He claimed to be God. He said that he had always existed. He told Nicodemus that God sent him into the world "that the world might be saved through him" (John 3:17). If Jesus wasn't God, as he claimed, he was crazy to say such things.

Some, though, say that Jesus really never said such things, that the Gospel writers wrote those things decades after Jesus died. Sometimes one even hears that Jesus never claimed to be God.

Usually, though, these people acknowledge that Jesus claimed to forgive sins. He did this frequently. Once was during the dinner given by Simon the Pharisee when a sinful woman bathed Jesus' feet with her tears and wiped them with her hair. He told her, "Your sins are forgiven" (Luke 7:48). The others at table said to themselves, "Who is this who even forgives sins?" (Luke 7:49).

Perhaps even a better example is the healing of a paralytic, reported by Matthew, Mark and Luke. When the paralytic was lowered down from the roof of the house Jesus was in, Jesus first said to him, "Your sins are forgiven." According to Mark (Chapter 2), the scribes sitting there understood Jesus' claim, for they asked, "Why does this man speak that way? He is blaspheming. Who but God alone can forgive sins?"

When Jesus healed the paralytic, he told those scribes specifically that he was doing it "that you may know that the Son of Man has authority to forgive sins on earth" (Mark 2:10). If only God can forgive sins, Jesus obviously claimed to be God.

As a man, I can forgive you for injuring me, but I have no right to forgive you for injuring someone else. If you sin by breaking God's laws, only God can forgive that. And Jesus claimed to have the authority to do that.

As is frequently the case, C. S. Lewis wrote as clearly as anyone else about Jesus' claim to be divine. In the chapter titled "The Shocking Alternative" in his book *Mere Christianity* he wrote: "I am trying to prevent anyone saying the really foolish thing that people often say about (Jesus): 'I'm ready to accept Jesus as a great moral teacher, but I don't accept His claim to be God.' That is the one thing we must not say. A man who was merely a man and said the sort of things Jesus said would not be a great moral teacher. He would either be a lunatic—on a level with the man who says he is a poached egg—or else he would be the Devil of Hell. You must make your choice. Either this man was, and is, the Son of God, or else a madman or something worse. You can shut him up for a fool, you can spit at him and kill him as a demon; or you can fall at his feet and call him Lord and God. But let us not come with any patronizing nonsense about his being a great human teacher. He has not left that open to us. He did not intend to."

But why is the divinity of Christ so important? We'll tackle the answer to that question in our next chapter.

CHAPTER 8

ONLY GOD COULD ATONE FOR SINS

In the previous chapter, I tried to make the case that it is not sufficient for Christians to follow Christ just because he was a great man. He claimed to be God, forgave sins (which only God can do), and performed healing miracles to show that he had the power to forgive sins.

But why is the divinity of Christ so important for Catholics? After all, many people who call themselves Christians believe that he was simply a great moral teacher without acknowledging him as God. It's almost like they forget that Jesus accepted death by crucifixion to atone for our sins and to redeem humankind.

Atonement and redemption are at the very core of Catholicism. As Catholics we believe that Jesus, the Second Person of the Blessed Trinity, became human in order to die for our sins. Our faith is as simple as that.

I guess most Christian religions teach that, but they differ on exactly what that means. Through the centuries of Christianity, people have questioned why atonement and redemption were necessary. Various churches have answered that question differently, but, as we saw in Chapter 4, the Catholic Church maintains the traditional doctrine of original sin.

Although churches differ on the doctrine of original sin, most Christians accept the fact that human nature was in a fallen state prior to Christ's death. Most Christians accept the words of the Nicene Creed, "For our sake he was crucified under Pontius Pilate; he suffered death and was buried." They also accept the words of Saint Paul in his First Letter to the Corinthians: "Christ died for our sins in accordance with the Scriptures" (15:3).

26

And that's why the divinity of Christ is so important. How could any mere man, even the holiest, die for our sins? How could a mere man be crucified "for our sake"? Our redemption had to be accomplished by God.

But not by God alone. Since suffering and death were part of God's plan, God couldn't do it by himself since it is not in God's nature to suffer and die. So first he had to assume our human nature; he had to become a human who could suffer and die. And that's what he did. God the Son became a man while remaining God and, in the person of Jesus, was able to make the perfect sacrifice that atoned for our sins.

Saint Paul, having already told us how sin entered the world, also told us, "Just as through the disobedience of one person the many were made sinners, so through the obedience of one the many will be made righteous" (Romans 5:19).

Saint Peter wrote: "He himself bore our sins in his body upon the cross, so that, free from sin, we might live for righteousness. By his wounds you have been healed" (1 Peter 2:24).

The *United States Catholic Catechism for Adults* puts it this way: "On the Cross, Jesus freely gave his life as a sacrifice. His sacrifice was an act of atonement, that is, it makes us one again with God by the power of divine mercy extending to us the Father's forgiveness of our sins."

It's true that, historically, certain Jewish authorities wanted Jesus to be put to death and handed him over to the Romans who governed Palestine at the time. But Catholics today do not blame all of the Jewish people for Christ's death. The *Catechism of the Catholic Church* says, "The Church does not hesitate to impute to Christians the gravest responsibility for the torments inflicted upon Jesus, a responsibility with which they have all too often burdened the Jews alone" (No. 598).

The Apostles' Creed says that, after his death, Jesus descended into hell. What does that mean? Why would he go to hell? Well, this was not the hell where Catholics believe the devil lives. This was the name the early Church used for the realm of the dead. Jesus went there after his death to wake up the just people who had died since Adam's sin so they could enter heaven. He had achieved their redemption.

CHAPTER 9

THE RESURRECTION

Back in 1998 in Lee County, Fla., there was a lot of hullabaloo about a Bible course being taught in the public school. Opponents said that it was OK to teach the Old Testament as history, but they objected to teaching the New Testament because the resurrection of Jesus was being taught as historical fact rather than religious belief. (The course was modified enough to meet with their approval.)

Catholics, of course, are convinced that the Resurrection *is* historical fact. Christianity, in fact, is based on that historical fact. Saint Paul wrote to the Corinthians, "If Christ has not been raised, your faith is vain" (1 Corinthians 15:17).

It's easy to understand how people without faith can doubt the Resurrection. It just isn't within our modern sphere of experience. Well, it wasn't within the Apostles' sphere of experience either. Our belief in the Resurrection is helped by the fact that the Apostles doubted it. They weren't gullible men who easily accepted something like a man coming back from the dead.

As often as Jesus predicted that he would rise from the dead, the Gospels make it clear that the Apostles didn't understand what he was talking about. They didn't even believe the women who went to the tomb. It took Jesus' appearance to them before they believed. These were simple men, to be sure, but not gullible or naïve. They just couldn't fathom that someone could actually rise from the dead.

People today who don't believe that Jesus actually rose from the dead must think that the first Christians were awfully naïve to believe such a thing. Either that or extremely clever to be able to concoct such a story and then sell it not only to their fellow Jews but also to Gentiles all over the world. The fact that the Apostles refused to believe at first shows that they were not naïve, and Gospel accounts of the Apostles show that they were hardly the type of men who could plan and carry out a gigantic fraud.

The news about Jesus' resurrection from the dead spread by word of mouth for decades before it was put down on paper. It was Saint Paul who first did that, in a letter he wrote in the year 56 from Ephesus, in modern Turkey, to the community he started in Corinth, Greece. This was about twenty-six years after Jesus' resurrection but still before any of the Gospels were written.

In that letter, Paul reminded his readers what he had preached: "that Christ died for our sins in accordance with the Scriptures; that he was buried; that he was raised on the third day in accordance with the Scriptures; that he appeared to Kephas [Peter], then to the Twelve. After that, he appeared to more than five hundred brothers at once, most of whom are still living, though some have fallen asleep. After that he appeared to James, then to the apostles. Last of all, as to one born abnormally, he appeared to me" (1 Corinthians 5:3-8).

That was then, and is now, the basic teaching of Christianity about Christ's resurrection. Paul was quite insistent about it when he wrote to the Corinthians, saying that our very salvation depends upon the fact that Jesus rose from the dead. Christians are not given a choice in deciding whether or not to believe in the Resurrection.

Some people confuse resurrection with resuscitation. Christians do not believe that Jesus was only resuscitated as he himself resuscitated Lazarus, the son of the widow of Nain, and the daughter of Jairus. Jesus rose from the dead with a glorified body, one that could pass through the locked doors where the Apostles stayed, one that could appear to the disciples on the road to Emmaus and could just as quickly disappear. And yet it was Jesus' body, one that Thomas could touch when he was invited to examine Jesus' wounds.

Christian faith in the Resurrection has met with incomprehension and opposition from the beginning. In the early fifth century, the great Saint Augustine wrote, "On no point does the Christian faith encounter more opposition than on the resurrection of the body." Yet it has always been, and remains today, the cornerstone of the Christian faith.

CHAPTER 10

JESUS AS PERSONAL SAVIOR

Yes, we Catholics do take Jesus Christ as our personal savior.

I wanted to make that point at the start of this chapter because some people seem to think that we don't. Perhaps it's the image they have of Catholics with rosary beads or saints' medals. They know that Catholics (and members of Orthodox churches) often have a greater devotion to Mary than do Protestants. Maybe that's why they have the impression that Jesus can get lost in the shuffle.

Actually, every devotion in the Catholic Church must lead directly to Jesus or it's not truly Catholic. As Pope John Paul II wrote in his best-selling book *Crossing the Threshold of Hope*, "From the beginning Christ has been at the center of the faith and life of the Church, and also at the center of her teaching and theology."

He also wrote, "A Marian dimension and Mariology in the Church are simply another aspect of the Christological focus." In other words, devotion to Mary must help us focus on Jesus Christ. I'll say more about that in the chapter about devotion to Mary.

What we Catholics believe about Jesus is summarized in both the Apostles' Creed and the Nicene Creed. In the former we say that we believe that Jesus was God's only Son and that he "was conceived by the Holy Spirit, born of the virgin Mary, suffered under Pontius Pilate, was crucified, died and was buried. He descended into hell. The third day he rose again from the dead. He ascended into heaven and is seated at the right hand of God the Father Almighty. From thence he will come to judge the living and the dead."

The Nicene Creed, which Catholics recite every Sunday during Mass, is a bit more technical. Composed in the fourth century, this creed affirms that we believe in "one Lord, Jesus Christ, the only Son of God, eternally begotten of the Father, . . . consubstantial with the Father. Through him all things were made."

Then come the parts that pertain to Jesus as savior. We say that we believe that "for us and for our salvation he came down from heaven. By the power of the Holy Spirit he was born of the virgin Mary, and became man. For our sake he was crucified under Pontius Pilate." The rest is similar to the Apostles' Creed.

We Catholics, therefore, believe that Jesus is our personal savior, that the reason he suffered and died was for our salvation. The goal of salvation is union with God, the heavenly life, and the consummation of our happiness as human beings. We believe, as is stated in the Acts of the Apostles, that "there is no salvation through anyone else, nor is there any other name under heaven given to the human race by which we are to be saved" (Acts 4:12).

Jesus died in accordance with his Father's will, to save us from our sins. It is now up to us to take advantage of the graces he has gained for us to complete our salvation.

Unlike some Protestants, though, Catholics do not believe that our salvation is assured once we accept Jesus as our personal savior. We must cooperate with the graces that come from God through the Church and live our lives in accordance with the teachings of Christ's Church.

CHAPTER 11

OLD HERESIES NEVER DIE

Here in the twenty-first century, two thousand years after Jesus lived on the earth, Christians are still trying to figure out just who he was. In the process many of them, Catholics and Protestants, could be considered heretics.

That thought came to me originally while I was researching and writing a two-volume work on the Doctors of the Church. They are the thirty-one men and four women the Catholic Church has designated its greatest teachers. All but nine of them lived prior to the Protestant Reformation when there was only one Western Christian Church. Thirteen of them lived in the fourth and fifth centuries, after Christians were able to come out of the catacombs. That's when Christian doctrine was being defined and errors, considered heresies, were being combated.

All of these "Doctors," as well as Church councils that defined what Christians are supposed to believe, taught that Jesus was both God and man, that he had both a divine and human nature but was only one person, that he always existed as God the Son, that he was equal to God the Father, that he was born as a human, that he died and rose again, that he ascended into heaven, and that he will come again.

The problems came in trying to decide how all that could be. Some very sincere men slipped into heresies when they tried to explain who Jesus was. And some of the ideas they came up with seem to continue today.

There still are those who believe that Jesus was a great man but deny that he was God. That's an obvious heresy since the doctrine of the

Incarnation—that the Second Person of the Trinity came to earth as a human without ceasing to be divine—is the very basis of Christianity.

Others believe that he was the Son of God but not really equal to God the Father. Despite what the Nicene Creed says ("begotten, not made"), they have the idea that God the Father created God the Son, which is the old heresy of Arianism.

Others don't think of God the Son as Creator, assigning that attribute solely to God the Father, again despite what the Creed says ("Through him all things were made") or what John's Gospel says ("All things came to be through him, and without him nothing came to be"). Some people, in fact, think of God the Creator, God the Redeemer, and God the Sanctifier as if there were three gods instead of one.

There are still Christians who believe that Mary was the mother only of Jesus the man and should not be called mother of God. That was the heresy of Nestorianism. But Christianity taught that Christ was only one person, not two. If Mary was the mother of that person and if that person was God, then Mary was the mother of God.

Today, too, it seems to me that many Christians question Jesus' complete humanity—the old heresy of Monophysitism. They give lip service to Saint Paul's statement that Jesus was "a man like us in all things but sin," but they have trouble thinking, for example, that he really was subject to illness or fatigue, all the humbling human bodily functions, or the sexual desires and temptations that all men have.

Those who think that Jesus was somehow not subject to all the things that make one a human might be guilty of Docetism, the heresy that taught that Christ merely assumed the appearance of a human body.

There are many other old heresies still around, but the ones I've mentioned concern Christ. Another popular heresy, especially among Americans, is Pelagianism, the belief that humans can obtain salvation solely through their own efforts.

It seems that old heresies never die. Nor, like old generals, do they fade away.

CHAPTER 12

THE HOLY SPIRIT

My first wife (she died in 2010 and I've remarried) once told me that, back when she was in a Catholic elementary school, her teacher polled her class with this question: "Which is the greatest or most important person of the Blessed Trinity—the Father, the Son, or the Holy Spirit?" Marie said that she was the only one who voted for the Holy Spirit. She said that she knew the others would vote for the Father or the Son and she felt sorry for the Holy Spirit.

It was a trick question. None of the three persons is greater or more important; they are all equal. All three persons of the Blessed Trinity are God, the three persons in one God.

In the Nicene Creed we say, "We believe in the Holy Spirit, the Lord, the giver of life, who proceeds from the Father and the Son. With the Father and the Son he is worshiped and glorified." Thus we proclaim belief in the Holy Spirit in precisely the same way in which we proclaim belief in the Father and the Son.

What does it mean that the Holy Spirit "proceeds" from the Father and the Son? Theologians explain that the Son is the Word of the Father, eternally begotten. The Father and the Son love each other with an eternal love. This love that proceeds from the Father and the Son is a person, the eternal Holy Spirit. I realize that not many Catholics understand what "proceeds" means when they recite the Creed, but perhaps you can remember that the Holy Spirit is the personification of the love that proceeds between the Father and the Son.

Since the Holy Spirit is God, he was with the Father at the time of creation, although we usually attribute the act of creation to the Father.

The Holy Spirit was also with the Son in his act of redemption. And the Holy Spirit is called the sanctifier for his actions on us through the sacraments of the Church.

The Holy Spirit was present in Old Testament times, even though the mystery of the Trinity was not revealed to God's Chosen People. When we say in the Nicene Creed that the Holy Spirit "has spoken through the prophets," we profess our belief that he inspired the Jewish prophets in their prophecies. They often referred to the working of the Spirit of God, using the Hebrew word *Ruah*, meaning "breath" and "the source of life." We also believe that the Holy Spirit inspired the authors of the Old Testament.

But the Old Testament does not speak of the Holy Spirit as a divine person distinct from the Father. It's in the New Testament that we learn most about the Holy Spirit, in all four Gospels, in the Acts of the Apostles, and in Saint Paul's letters.

In John's Gospel, Jesus promised to send "another paraclete." The word "paraclete" means "counselor" or "advocate." We believe that God had to have a plan whereby Christ's teachings would be preserved after Christ was no longer in the world. That is why he sent the Holy Spirit, to lead the Church and preserve it from error.

After the Resurrection, John tells us that Jesus breathed on the apostles and said, "Receive the Holy Spirit. Whose sins you forgive are forgiven and whose sins you retain are retained" (John 20:22-23).

At Pentecost the Holy Spirit descended fully upon the Church and the Apostles were aware of his direct operation in their activities. The letters of Saint Paul show us that the Spirit had an important place in his theology, with his description of the many gifts of the Spirit.

The Holy Spirit has been called the "soul" of the Church, which is the body of Christ. The Church teaches that the gifts of Christ are poured out upon the Church by the Holy Spirit.

Besides keeping the Church from error, the Holy Spirit is also the communicator of grace to human beings. It's for that reason that he is called the sanctifier. Grace is a free gift of God, given to us through the merits of Christ and communicated to us by the Holy Spirit. It is divine assistance given to people to help them advance toward their supernatural destiny of fellowship with God. The principal means of grace are the sacraments, which I'll discuss in later chapters.

CHAPTER 13

DEVOTION TO MARY

One of the things Protestants don't understand about Catholics and Orthodox Christians is their strong devotion to Mary, the mother of Jesus. Catholics, by the same token, don't understand why Protestants don't have a greater devotion to her.

Catholics and Orthodox honor Mary because God himself did so by making her the mother of the Word, the Second Person of the Blessed Trinity. Luke's Gospel (1:48, 49) quotes Mary in her Magnificat as saying, "From now on will all ages call me blessed. The Mighty One has done great things for me." For Protestants who claim to follow Scripture alone, you'd think they would be quick to call Mary blessed and venerate her. She appears in the New Testament more than any other woman.

The objection that some Protestants have toward Catholic and Orthodox devotion to Mary is that this devotion seems to put Mary on the same level as Jesus. If this were true, it would be heretical. Neither the Catholic nor Orthodox Churches make Mary an equal with Jesus. They do not adore Mary. Mary's role is to lead us to her Son, to deepen our devotion to Jesus as the Christ, our Savior.

Catholics and Orthodox believe Mary is the greatest saint and they pray to her for her intercession with her Son. In the Hail Mary prayer, we ask Mary to "pray for us sinners now and at the hour of our death."

Here are the Catholic doctrines about Mary:

1. She is the mother of God. The Council of Ephesus in 431 solemnly established that Jesus had two natures, the divine and the human, but he was one person, and Mary was the mother of that person. If Jesus was God, as Christians believe, and Mary was his mother, then Mary was the

mother the God. It's a simply syllogism: Jesus was God; Mary was his mother; therefore, Mary was the mother of God.

2. Mary remained a virgin all her life. Both Luke's Gospel (1:35) and Matthew's (1:20) tell us that Mary conceived Jesus through the power of the Holy Spirit, while remaining a virgin. The conviction that she remained a virgin after Jesus' birth developed early in the church. As for the "brethren of Jesus" referred to in Scripture, Catholics believe either that they were cousins or, along with the Orthodox, that they were Joseph's children by a previous marriage. In this view, Joseph was an older widower who agreed to care for her. Some Protestants deny that Mary remained a virgin, although it's interesting to note that Martin Luther, John Calvin and John Wesley all held that she was ever-virgin.

3. Mary was conceived without original sin. This doctrine is called the Immaculate Conception and should not be confused with the doctrine of the virgin birth. It means that, when Mary was conceived by her parents, she was preserved from the sin that, according to Christian doctrine, we are all born with. This doctrine, not formally defined until 1854, states that Mary had a "preservative redemption" in anticipation of the foreseen merits of Jesus. The only biblical basis for this doctrine is the angel Gabriel's address to Mary, "Hail, full of grace" or, in modern translations, "Hail, highly favored one" (Luke 1:28). If Mary was full of grace, according to Catholic teaching, it meant that she did not have original sin on her soul.

4. Mary was assumed, body and soul, into heaven. This doctrine, called the Assumption, was not defined as dogma until 1950, but the feast of the Assumption was being celebrated as early as the sixth century. There is no biblical basis for this dogma.

Through the centuries, various saints had a great devotion to Mary and painters delighted in Madonna and Child paintings. She has always been seen as a loving friend in heaven and the mother of all who are born to life. The U.S. Catholic bishops, in a letter issued in 1976 titled "Behold Your Mother," appealed to the "basic reverence" of all Christians for Mary, "a veneration deeper than doctrinal differences and theological disputes."

CHAPTER 14

ANCIENT TRADITIONS ABOUT MARY

Here are some ancient traditions about Mary. Catholics do not have to believe in them all, but only the doctrines listed in the previous chapter. Early Christians, however, did believe them to be true.

Mary is believed to have been born in Jerusalem, near the Bethesda Pools. Her parents were Joachim and Anne. Today the Church of St. Anne, built by the Crusaders in the twelfth century, is over the site.

Joachim and Anne were elderly when Mary was born. When Mary was three, they took her to the Temple, as they promised to do before she was born, and left her there. Israeli researchers have discovered that this was not uncommon. Girls were raised in the Temple and given a thorough Torah education in exchange for performing various services for the priests.

These girls, though, had to leave the temple before puberty because menstruation made a woman ritually impure. Women could not be in the Temple when they were menstruating. Apparently Mary's parents had died by the time Mary reached adolescence, so the priests looked for a husband for her among widowers. An older man was sought for her husband because Mary had taken a vow of virginity. Her husband was expected to protect her and to honor her vow.

According to early documents, several widowers were gathered. A dove flew out of the rod of a carpenter from Nazareth named Joseph, and flew onto his head. This was taken as a sign that Joseph was to become Mary's husband. He protested that he was old and already had six children, but he agreed to take Mary as his wife. He would protect her while she helped him care for his children. The names of Joseph's four sons are in the

Gospels of Matthew (13:55) and Mark (6:3): James, Joseph, Judas and Simon. His daughters are not named.

None of the above traditions are in the Bible; they are traditions, not doctrine. The Gospels do, however, tell us about the appearance of an angel to Mary to ask her to become Jesus' mother without violating her vow of virginity, her acceptance, her visit to her relative Elizabeth, and the birth of Jesus in Bethlehem. The Gospels tell us about the presentation of Jesus in the Temple when he was forty days old, the flight into Egypt to escape King Herod, the family moving to the town of Nazareth, and the finding of Jesus in the Temple when he stayed there at the age of twelve.

Since Joseph was an older man, we believe that he died before Jesus began his public life. As a widow Mary was probably cared for by Joseph's older children, allowing Jesus to abandon his career as a carpenter when he began his public life.

Mary appears in the Gospels at the wedding feast of Cana and when she accompanied Jesus' brothers when they tried to take him back to Nazareth because they thought he was out of his mind.

She was at the foot of the cross when Jesus was crucified, according to John's Gospel. Luke's Gospel already established that Mary went to Jerusalem for the feast of Passover, so that is probably why she was in the city at the time. According to the Acts of the Apostles, she was also present when the Holy Spirit came upon those assembled in the Upper Room.

The building where the Upper Room was located became the first Christian church. Mary moved into a home across the street with the apostle John and probably her stepson James, the first bishop of Jerusalem. The Byzantine church Hagia Sion was built over her home in 415 and the Crusaders replaced it with the Santa Maria Church. Today the Dormition Abbey stands atop the excavations of those churches.

Mary died there and was buried in the Kidron Valley, near the Garden of Gethsemane. Catholics believe that from there she was taken bodily to heaven. Today the tomb is still venerated but all that is left is the empty crypt of a basilica built in the fourth century. Some Catholics, though, believe that she moved to Ephesus with the Apostle John and died there. It seems more likely, though, that John moved to Ephesus after Mary's death and assumption into heaven.

CHAPTER 15

CATHOLICS AND THE BIBLE

One of the differences between Protestantism and Catholicism is that some Catholic beliefs are not based on the Bible. Catholics believe that the Bible is the inspired word of God, but the Catholic faith is not based on the Bible. That's because the Catholic Church existed before the Bible. In fact, it was the Catholic Church that determined what books would be in the New Testament—even, for that matter what books would be in the Catholic version of the Old Testament.

The Bible has been called the greatest book ever written. It has had a profound influence on world civilization. But it is far more than just a book. We Catholics believe that through the Bible, God himself speaks to us. Although the Bible has human authors, we believe that ultimately it has only one author—God. He made use of the authors of Sacred Scripture to communicate revelation by means of inspiration from the Holy Spirit.

The earliest book of the New Testament was Saint Paul's First Letter to the Thessalonians, written about the year 51, roughly twenty years after Jesus' death and resurrection. The four Gospels were written roughly between 70 (Mark's) and 100 (John's).

Between the year 30, when Jesus ascended into heaven, and the writing of our present Gospels, many other writings about Jesus were composed. In fact, we have fragments of, or at least know about, nearly eighty such Gospels. Some of these were called *The Gospel of Thomas, The Gospel of Peter, The Infancy Gospel of Thomas, The Protevangelium of James, The Gospel of the Hebrews,* and *The Secret Gospel of Mark.*

With all these accounts available, it was up to the Church to determine which of them were authentic, and that's what it did over a long period of time. It accepted some books and rejected others, finally selecting the twenty-seven books that now appear in the New Testament at the Council of Carthage in 397. Today all Christians agree on those twenty-seven books.

Meanwhile, near the end of the first century, Jewish scholars were selecting the writings for their Scriptures, what Christians call the Old Testament. They eliminated any books that were not preserved in Hebrew—even the Books of Maccabees which gave them their feast of Hanukkah.

The Catholic Church, though, accepted those books as well as Tobit, Wisdom, Judith, Ecclesiasticus, Baruch and some additional passages in the books of Daniel and Esther. These were included in the Christian Bible until the Protestant Reformation in the sixteenth century, when the reformers went back to the list chosen by the Jewish scholars.

The difference between Catholic and Protestant Bibles, therefore, is not in the New Testament but the Old. There are seven more books in the Catholic Old Testament than there are in the Protestants'.

Because the Catholic Church predates the Bible, it accepts some traditions and doctrines that have come down through the centuries but are not specifically in the Bible. It has also had great theologians who have interpreted the Bible, men like Saints Augustine, Thomas Aquinas, Bonaventure, Athanasius, and Gregory the Great.

The Catholic Church also believes that, among the seventh-three books in its Bible, there are many literary genres. We should not read the Bible as history, and certainly not as a scientific book. There are even four novels in the Old Testament—specifically Jonah, Tobit, Esther and Judith. This is something that some fundamentalists do not accept. They fear that admitting that the Bible contains poetry, fiction and other literary forms is somehow an attack on the veracity of the Bible.

Roman Catholic teaching, on the other hand, as well as that of many other Christian denominations, sees no incompatibility between recognizing the truth of the biblical witness and the fact that it is expressed in many forms of literary expression. Poetry, hymns, stories, myths and other literary forms can communicate both historical and theological truth.

Nevertheless, the Catholic Church teaches that the Bible contains the words of God, expressed in the words of men. It is God's self-revelation, the communication of the mystery of God to the world. It is a sacred book that Catholics, and all others, are encouraged to read daily. Readings from the Bible are included in every Catholic Mass.

CHAPTER 16

ONE, HOLY, CATHOLIC
AND APOSTOLIC

This chapter is a bit more personal than the others. It's condensed from a talk I once gave on why I'm a Catholic.

I'm a Catholic because I've learned through the years that the Catholic Church is what it claims to be in the Nicene Creed: one, holy, catholic and apostolic.

It is one church in its teachings—always the same whether you're in the United States, Europe, South America, Asia, or anyplace else in the world. Every Catholic church is ultimately under the jurisdiction of the pope.

It is holy because it has the Eucharist and the other sacraments that help us to become holy. To receive the body and blood of Jesus is the ultimate in intimacy with God this side of heaven. I also appreciate the opportunities the Catholic Church makes available for those who want to become closer to God—to become holy—through prayer.

A mark of the Church's holiness is the large list of saints who have shown us how to follow Christ. These people found their holiness in the Catholic Church and we can do likewise. They are our role models as well as our intercessors.

I've discovered that the Church is catholic, or universal, through my travels. It really does exist everywhere in the world. I've gone to the same Mass in China, India, Russia, the Holy Land, places in South America and throughout Europe. The Catholic Church has both great diversity and unity in its universality.

The Catholic Church is apostolic. It alone can trace itself back to the Apostles. Many converts to Catholicism have been converted mainly for that reason. One of the most famous is Blessed John Henry Newman, who was a leader in the Anglican Church's Oxford Movement in the nineteenth century. He began to write a book showing that the Anglican Church was the *via media*—the middle way—between Catholicism and Protestantism. But as he studied the Church's history, he had to acknowledge that Catholicism was indeed the same Church founded by Christ and spread by the Apostles. Newman went on to become the greatest theologian in the Catholic Church in the nineteenth century. Eventually, he was named a cardinal.

The Church has had a checkered history, to say the least. But it has survived some simply awful popes in the fifteenth century who thought more of enriching their families than in being spiritual leaders, or who fathered illegitimate children and plotted to murder their opponents. There have been thirty-seven antipopes in the Church's history, men who claimed or exercised the papal office in an uncanonical manner. During one period of history, 1378 to 1417, there were two and sometimes three men claiming to be pope, each with followers who thought that their man was the legitimate pope. My feeling is that, if the Church could survive all of that, and more, it must be divinely protected in order to last all these centuries.

One, holy, catholic and apostolic—those are what we know as the four marks of the Church. There's also a fifth: The Catholic Church fosters and promotes devotion to Mary, the mother of God. I feel that only the Catholic and Orthodox Churches give to Mary the devotion to which she is entitled.

I'm a Catholic because I accept the teachings of the Catholic Church. Although the basic truths of the Catholic faith are included in the Creed that Catholics recite during Mass each Sunday, Catholics are expected to believe many other things, too. These things range from doctrines like the Immaculate Conception and Assumption of Mary, to controversial issues like the restriction of ordination to celibate men and to questions about sexual morality.

When I have difficulties I'm comforted by the words of Cardinal Newman, whom I've already said was the greatest theologian of the nineteenth century. He wrote for those having difficulty with a particular doctrine of the Church, "Ten thousand difficulties do not make one doubt."

I also remind myself that the Catholic Church has existed for nearly two thousand years, during which it has constantly preserved the faith it received from the Apostles. During that time, too, thousands of brilliant men and women, much smarter than I, have accepted the Church's teachings. How could I do anything less?

CHAPTER 17

BELIEF IN TRADITION

In Chapter 15, I wrote that, while Catholics believe that the Bible is the inspired word of God, the Catholic faith is not based solely on the Bible. I had better elaborated on that because it is sometimes confusing both to Catholics and to others.

Catholics believe that God has transmitted divine revelation to us in two distinct modes: Scripture and tradition. The Gospel of Christ was handed on in two ways: first, orally by the Apostles, who were inspired by the Holy Spirit to preach, and, later, in writing by those who were also inspired by the Holy Spirit to commit the message of salvation to writing.

The disciples of Jesus were spreading the faith through their preaching, as Christ commanded them to do, for about twenty years before the first New Testament writing appeared: Paul's Letters to the Thessalonians. In one of those letters Paul advises those to whom he was writing: "Therefore, brothers, stand firm and hold fast to the traditions that you were taught, either by an oral statement or by a letter of ours" (2 Thessalonians: 2:15).

The early Christians followed those traditions that Paul wrote about well before the first Gospel was written about forty years after Christ's resurrection. And those traditions are an integral part of Catholic faith.

When the Catholic Church uses the word "tradition," it means more than just custom, as in, "That's the way we've always done it; it's a tradition." The word comes from the Latin, meaning "handing over," and it means the teachings and practices that were handed over by the Apostles to their successors. This is known as the "deposit of faith."

When, before his ascension to heaven, Jesus commissioned his Apostles to make disciples of all nations, he told them, "I am with you always, until the end of the age" (Matthew 28:20). He obviously expected his teachings to be continued long after the Apostles were dead. Therefore, the Apostles entrusted the deposit of faith to the Church that Jesus founded upon Peter. The task of preserving, spreading and interpreting the deposit of faith was given to the Apostles' successors, the bishops, in communion with the successors of Peter, the bishop of Rome.

The immediate successors of the Apostles included those who are known as the Apostolic Fathers, men like Saint Polycarp, a disciple of Saint John, and Saint Irenaeus, a disciple of Polycarp. Others were Saint Clement of Rome and Saint Ignatius of Antioch. They and their successors, under the inspiration of the Holy Spirit, handed on the deposit of faith.

As followers of Christ began to write the Gospels, it was the Apostles' successors who had to determine which of them were inspired by the Holy Spirit. Besides the writings that now make up the New Testament, there were many other works that purported to come from Peter, John, James, Thomas, Philip, Mary Magdalene, Barnabas, and others. Local churches had different "canons," lists of accepted books. It was important to determine which were authentic.

The Muratorian Canon, from about 150, is the oldest surviving canon. But it wasn't until 367 that Saint Athanasius, the bishop of Alexandria, became the first to declare the twenty-seven books of the New Testament as the canon binding on the whole Church. This was reaffirmed by the North African Synod of Carthage in 419, but the matter wasn't conclusively settled until the ecumenical Council of Trent in the sixteenth century.

Today Catholics believe that Scripture and tradition together make up a single sacred deposit of the word of God.

CHAPTER 18

THE POPE IS NOT INFALLIBLE

Many people are confused by what the Catholic Church teaches about infallibility. For example, to the surprise of many, it does not believe that the pope is infallible. Many people think that the Catholic Church does teach that, and it has been a stumbling block for ecumenism, but the actual teaching is more nuanced.

"Infallibility" is a double-negative word meaning "the inability to err." It's not the same as "being correct" because someone could be correct without being *necessarily* correct. Infallibility for humans is possible only with divine assistance.

The Catholic Church believes that Jesus promised that divine assistance to Peter and the other Apostles when he said, "Thou art Peter and upon this rock I will build my Church . . . . I will give you the keys to the kingdom of heaven. Whatever you bind on earth shall be bound in heaven; and whatever you loose on earth shall be loosed in heaven" (Matthew 16: 18-19).

The infallibility of the pope was debated during the First Vatican Council, in 1870. Some of the bishops, led by Archbishop Henry Edward Manning of England, thought that the pope was personally infallible, that he could not err. Others, led by Lord Acton and John Henry Newman, thought that the pope could make decisions binding on the whole Church only when he acted in agreement with the other bishops.

After lengthy discussion, a compromise was reached and the debate focused on the infallibility of the pope's doctrinal decisions rather than on the infallibility of the pope himself. Finally the council decreed that the pope teaches infallibly under three conditions: when he exercises his office as pastor of all Christians (known as *ex cathedra* or "from the chair" of Saint Peter), when he teaches on matters of faith or morals, and when he indicates that the doctrine must be held by the universal Church.

This is a subtle distinction between the infallibility of the pope himself and the infallibility of what he teaches, but it was considered an important distinction. Plus, not everything the pope teaches is infallible, but only what he teaches under those three conditions. When Pope Benedict XVI (now Pope Emeritus Benedict) wrote his best-selling book *Jesus of Nazareth*, he made it clear that people were free to disagree with his analyses and conclusions. He was not attempting to teach infallibly.

The Second Vatican Council, in 1964, elaborated on the doctrine of infallibility. It stated that the divine Redeemer willed that his Church should be endowed with infallibility when it comes to the deposit of divine revelation. It made it clear that, when the pope proclaims definitions of doctrines, they are pronounced with the assistance of the Holy Spirit promised to Peter and that, therefore, they need no approval of others.

But infallibility, the Second Vatican Council said, resides not only in the pope but also in the body of bishops "when that body exercises supreme teaching authority with the successor of Peter." The bishops of the Catholic Church, in union with the pope, have supreme teaching and pastoral authority over the whole Church in addition to the authority of office they have for their own dioceses.

The bishops' infallible teaching authority has been exercised in twenty-one councils through the centuries, most recently the Second Vatican Council in the 1960s. Doctrines concerning faith and morals defined by councils, after they have been promulgated by the pope, are considered to be infallible. That is how most doctrines have been defined.

Popes rarely speak *ex cathedra*. Usually, in talks, letters, books, and other ways, they state authentic teachings of the Catholic Church in line with Scripture, tradition, and the living experience of the Church. However, Catholics are expected to submit their wills and minds to the pope's teaching authority whether or not he is speaking infallibly.

Bishops, too, seldom exercise infallibility. But again Catholics are expected to accept bishops' teachings with religious assent.

CHAPTER 19

RESURRECTION OF THE BODY

From the beginning of time, humans have been concerned about death and about what happens afterward. Indeed, humans are the only animals who can think about that. We know that the ancient Egyptians buried their pharaohs with all the things they thought they might need in the next life. Some ancient peoples buried wives and servants with their kings, believing that they would need them in the next life.

For those who fear death, religion is consoling. But religious teachings about life after death vary considerably depending upon whether one is a Hindu, a Buddhist, a Jew, a Christian, or a member of another religion.

Catholics, indeed all Christians who recite the Nicene Creed, say that we believe in the resurrection of the body or the resurrection of the dead. It's a belief that has been an essential ingredient of the Christian faith from its beginnings. We are called to believe not only that the immortal soul will live on after our death but that even the mortal body will come to life again and be reunited with the soul. Saint Paul wrote to the Romans, "If the Spirit of the one who raised Jesus from the dead dwells in you, the one who raised Christ from the dead will give life to your mortal bodies also, through his Spirit that dwells in you" (Romans 8:11).

Saint Paul berated the Corinthians because some of them said that there was no resurrection of the dead. He wrote in his First Letter to the Corinthians, "If there is no resurrection of the dead, then Christ has not been raised; if Christ has not been raised, then our preaching is in vain and your faith is in vain" (15:14).

In Christ's day, not all Jews believed in the resurrection of the body, although some Jews believed in it at least as far back as the Maccabees.

During their persecution, the Maccabean martyrs told their persecutors, "The King of the universe will raise us up to an everlasting renewal of life, because we have died for his laws" (2 Maccabees 7:9).

Jesus definitely believed in, and taught, the resurrection of the body. He supported the Pharisees, who believed in life after death, in their dispute over this issue with the Sadducees, who did not believe in it. We Catholics believe that Jesus himself will raise up those who have believed in him. In John's Gospel, he told Martha, "I am the resurrection and the life; whoever believes in me, even if he dies, will live" (John 11:25).

Nevertheless, Christian faith in the resurrection has always met with opposition. In the fifth century, Saint Augustine wrote, "On no point does the Christian faith encounter more opposition than on the resurrection of the body."

How, skeptics ask, can a body that has decayed after death possibly be reunited with the soul? Other than believing that we will then possess a "spiritual body," rather than a corruptible body, we have to say that we don't know how God will accomplish that. The *United States Catholic Catechism for Adults* says, "The manner of our resurrection exceeds our understanding and imagination and is accessible only to our faith" (page 156).

The resurrection of the body will happen at the end of time, but our souls will enjoy their reward, or punishment, immediately after death. The Church calls this "the particular judgment" to distinguish it from the "last judgment." Jesus told us what the last judgment will be like. In the twenty-fifth chapter of the Gospel according to Saint Matthew, he says that he will judge us according to how well we fed the hungry, gave drink to the thirsty, clothed the naked, etc. It will display God's justice in condemning sinners and rewarding those who are saved.

The souls of those who have lived a life of faith will be reunited with the souls of friends and relatives in the community of heaven where they will see God as he is and enjoy supreme, and eternal, happiness.

That is the promise of our Catholic faith.

CHAPTER 20

HEAVEN AND HELL

After the final judgment, when our bodies are reunited with our souls, we will go either to heaven or to hell for all eternity.

Heaven is the state of being in which all are united in love with one another and with God, where those who, having attained salvation, are in glory with God and enjoy the beatific vision—knowledge of God as he is. It's the ultimate end and fulfillment of the deepest human longings, the state of supreme, definitive happiness.

In heaven, Saint John tells us, we shall become like God himself because we shall see him face to face. Or as Saint Thomas Aquinas wrote, "God became man so that man might become God."

The bliss of heaven will consist in what the Church calls two dimensions: the vertical dimension that is the vision and love of God, and the horizontal dimension that is the knowledge and love of all others in God. We will be reunited with our family and friends as well as with the saints from past, and future, generations.

We will experience perfect happiness in heaven. All of our deepest human longings will be fulfilled. Yet some people, because of their lives on earth, will experience greater happiness than others will. This will happen because some people will be given a greater capacity for happiness than others, depending upon their lives on earth. Just as both a large glass and a small glass can be filled to capacity but one will hold more than the other, so will some people have a greater capacity for happiness than others will. This is why we shouldn't just try to get into heaven by doing the bare minimum here on earth.

When it gets right down to it, we humans cannot understand heaven. What we know, though, is that "no eye has seen, nor ear heard, nor has the heart of man conceived, what God has prepared for those who love him" (1 Corinthians 2:9).

That brings us to hell. Yes, the Church teaches us that there really is a hell, certainly the least palatable of all the Church's doctrines. There are too many references to hell in Scripture to just pretend that hell doesn't exist. It's a place of eternal damnation for those who used the freedom God gave to them to reject God's love. It's the state of persons who die in mortal sin, in a condition of self-alienation from God.

Pope John Paul II asked, "Is not hell in a certain sense the ultimate safeguard of man's moral conscience?" How else is human freedom to be respected if it doesn't include the right to say no to God? We believe that God gives everyone the graces necessary to accept God's love and live according to his precepts, but he also gives everyone the freedom to reject that love.

Two questions about hell need to be addressed: the exact nature of the sufferings inflicted and the number of those condemned to endure them. Perhaps this statement from the German bishops' conference sums up the answer to the first question. They wrote: "Just as heaven is God himself won forever, so hell is God himself eternally lost. The essence of hell is final exclusion from communion with God because of one's own fault."

But what about the fires of hell we see in so many cartoons? This is a metaphor for the pain of eternal separation from God, which must be the most horrifying pain of all. There won't be physical fire, which wouldn't affect a spiritual body anyway.

And who is in hell? That's an ancient controversy because some theologians have taught that perhaps everyone will be saved, the concept of universal salvation.

Pope Paul II said at his general audience on July 28, 1999, "Eternal damnation remains a real possibility, but we are not granted . . . the knowledge of whether, or which, human beings are effectively involved in it." The Church has said infallibly, through the process of canonization, that certain people are in heaven, but it has never said that certain people are in hell.

CHAPTER 21

PURGATORY

One of the most common criticisms that Protestants have about the Catholic faith is our belief in purgatory. Protestants always want to know why we believe in purgatory even though it's not mentioned in the Bible.

The Catholic doctrine of purgatory is misunderstood not only by Protestants, but also by many Catholics. For example, they sometimes think of it as a place somewhere between heaven and hell, and it is not. Purgatory is the name given to a process of purification, not to a place the soul might go to after death.

Purgatory is part of Catholic teachings about heaven. That doctrine was formally defined by Pope Benedict XII on January 29, 1336. It read in part: "The souls of all the saints . . . and other faithful who died after receiving Christ's holy baptism (provided they were not in need of purification when they died, . . . or, if they then did need or will need some purification, when they have been purified after death . . .), already before they take up their bodies again and before the general judgment . . . have been, are and will be in heaven, in the heavenly kingdom and celestial paradise with Christ . . . . These souls have seen and do see the divine essence with an intuitive vision, and even face to face, without the mediation of any creature."

Sacred Scripture says that nothing impure will enter the kingdom of heaven. But you and I know that not everyone who dies is worthy to enter into perfect and complete union with God. Nor has he or she rejected God's mercy enough to sentence himself or herself to hell. In the process of purification we call purgatory, every trace of sin is eliminated and every imperfection is corrected.

The Catholic Church doesn't say when this will occur since the concept of time is meaningless in eternity. Perhaps it occurs immediately after death or even in the process of dying. We don't know.

Unfortunately, some pious folklore has made purgatory seem like a mini-hell where people spend years and years of torture and pain before finally being allowed into heaven. That, though, is not Catholic teaching. As Pope John Paul II said August 4, 1999, "Those who live in this state of purification after death are not separated from God but are immersed in the love of Christ."

Part of the problem of understanding purgatory is the belief that we, the relatives and friends of the deceased, can assist those who have died with our prayers. This is part of the doctrine of the communion of saints that we say we believe in when we recite the Apostles' Creed.

Pope John Paul alluded to this in the same address when he said that the souls in purgatory are not separated from the saints in heaven or from us on earth. "We all remain united in the Mystical Body of Christ," he said, "and we can therefore offer up prayers and good works on behalf of our brothers and sisters in purgatory."

Belief in the efficacy of prayers for the dead goes back at least as far as the Second Book of Maccabees (12:39-46). After Judas had won a battle he found that dead Jewish soldiers had committed a sin by wearing idolatrous amulets under their tunics. He and his men "prayed that the sinful deed might be fully blotted out." Then they took up a collection which he sent to Jerusalem for an expiatory sacrifice. "Thus he made atonement for the dead that they might be freed from this sin," the chapter concludes.

Thus, although the process of purgatory isn't mentioned in the Bible, the idea of prayers for the dead that they might be cleansed from their sins is. (Admittedly, though, the Second Book of Maccabees is considered an apocryphal book in Protestant Bibles.)

CHAPTER 22

INDULGENCES

Readers might be surprised that I'm including a chapter about indulgences in this book. I can imagine the reaction of both Catholics and Protestants: "Indulgences? I thought the Catholic Church ended them a long time ago."

It's true that Catholics haven't heard much about indulgences in recent decades, and the only thing that most Protestants know about them is that Martin Luther started his reformation because of them. Perhaps I should have just ignored them for this book because they're too divisive.

Yet, the Catholic Church does still grant indulgences. And yes, they are widely misunderstood by both Catholics and those of other faiths. There will undoubtedly continue to be disagreements about them, but at least we can understand what the Catholic Church actually teaches about them.

An indulgence is not the forgiveness of sins, either past or future. In the simplest terms, an indulgence is the remission of the temporal punishment due for sins whose guilt has already been forgiven. It can be either partial or plenary, depending on whether it does away with either part or all of the punishment due for sins. One gains indulgences through prayers, penance and good works in atonement, or reparation, for the sins that were forgiven.

The American legal system has something similar. Sometimes a judge will sentence someone who has committed a crime to so many hours of community service. The good work the criminal does helps atone for the evil that he or she committed.

Of course, for indulgences to make sense, you have to accept the Catholic concept of sin. The Catholic Church teaches that sin has a double consequence: an eternal punishment that, for grave sin, deprives us of communion with God, and a temporal punishment that must be purified either here on earth or after death in the state of purification known as purgatory. I explained the Catholic belief in purgatory in the previous chapter.

The forgiveness of sins in the sacrament of penance, or confession, remits the eternal punishment and restores our communion with God, but the temporal punishment remains. Indulgences, which the church attaches to works of mercy and various forms of penance, remit the temporal punishment.

The Catholic Church also teaches that indulgences can be gained both for oneself and for those who have died and who might still be in a state of purification before they can enter heaven. As I said in the previous chapter, this is part of the doctrine of the communion of saints that Christians profess to believe when they recite the Creed. Of course, the actual disposition of indulgences applied to the dead rests with God.

How can the Church decide that a certain practice—say, a visit to a church and prayers for the intentions of the pope—will remit temporal punishments due to sin? The Church believes that it can do that by virtue of its power of binding and loosing granted by Jesus. It can open for Christians what is known as the Church's treasury—not material goods but the infinite value which Christ's merits have before God.

Speaking of treasure and material goods, indulgences cannot be bought. No one can buy his or her, or a departed loved one's, way into heaven. That is what was happening during Martin Luther's time and he was correct in calling it an abuse. The German priest Johann Tetzel was raising money for the construction of Saint Peter's Basilica in Rome by telling people that they could obtain indulgences by making a contribution. This abuse is what prompted Luther to nail his ninety-five theses to the church door of Wittenburg on October 31, 1517.

CHAPTER 23

ANGELS

It's surprising how fashionable angels have become in our secular society. From popular television shows to jewelry to books, there seems to be a widespread interest in these messengers from God sent to help us humans.

Unfortunately, many people might acknowledge an interest in angels but will quickly say, "But, of course, I don't really believe in them."

Why not? I think a disbelief in angels is a form of pride. How do we dare to believe that there couldn't be a higher order of creatures than humans? Because we can't prove their existence scientifically? Because the idea of angels seems like myth?

Most religions do teach the real existence of angels. It's part of the traditional beliefs of Judaism, Christianity and Islam. The *Catechism of the Catholic Church*, for example, says, "The existence of the spiritual, non-corporeal beings that Sacred Scripture usually calls 'angels' is a truth of faith. The witness of Scripture is as clear as the unanimity of Tradition" (No. 328).

The word "angel," by the way, is the name of their office or function, not of their nature. Saint Augustine taught that the name of their nature is "spirit" because they are purely spiritual creatures. They have intelligence and free will and they surpass in perfection all visible creatures. Their mission is to serve as servants and messengers of God.

Angels have traditionally been assigned to nine "choirs": angels, archangels, principalities, powers, virtues, dominions, thrones, cherubim and seraphim.

Scriptures give us the names of only three angels: archangels Michael, Raphael and Gabriel, although Jewish apocrypha add Uriel and Jeremiel.

Michael first appears in Daniel's vision as "the great prince" who defends Israel against its enemies. In the Book of Revelation he leads God's armies to final victory over the forces of evil.

Raphael's only appearance is in the story of Tobit where he guides Tobiah through a series of fantastic adventures and heals Tobit's blindness.

Gabriel also makes an appearance in Daniel's visions, announcing Michael's role. He then appears in the New Testament, first to announce the birth of John the Baptist and then, his best-known appearance, to Mary, who consents to give birth to Jesus. Muslims believe that Gabriel appeared to Muhammad over a period of twenty years and dictated what was to become the Koran.

Unnamed angels appear throughout Jewish Scripture and the Christian Old Testament: They closed the earthly paradise, protected Lot, saved Hagar and her child, stayed Abraham's hand when he was going to sacrifice Isaac, communicated the law by their ministry, and assisted the prophets, just to cite a few examples.

The Second Book of Kings tells us that, when Sennacherib and his Assyrian forces were about to conquer Jerusalem, "the angel of the Lord went forth and struck down one hundred and eighty-five thousand men in the Assyrian camp" (19:35), persuading Sennacherib to return to Assyria.

The Gospels tell us that angels ministered to Jesus during various times in his life. They protected him in his infancy, served him in the desert, and strengthened him in his agony in the garden.

As for the Guardian Angels, their existence has never been explicitly defined as a matter of faith for Catholics, but belief in them goes back at least as far as Saint Basil the Great, who died in 379. He wrote, "Beside each believer stands an angel as protector and shepherd leading him to life."

Angels might not be as they are portrayed on TV, but they do exist.

CHAPTER 24

DEVOTION TO SAINTS

One of the ways the Catholic Church differs from other religions is its devotion to saints. It has honored people who lived heroically holy lives since the beginning of Christianity when it began to venerate Saint Stephen as the first martyr. For centuries local churches remembered holy people after their deaths, calling them saints and praying to them to ask for their intercession with God. Finally, the popes reserved for themselves the right to declare someone a saint.

The penchant for declaring people to be saints, known as canonization, definitely did not decline during the pontificate of Pope John Paul II. He canonized more people than all the other popes combined. Pope Benedict XVI didn't canonize as many as his predecessors did, but his pontificate was shorter. These is every indication that Pope Francis will continue to canonize saints at about the same rates as Pope John Paul II.

The Catholic Church canonizes people not only to honor them—they couldn't care less, being in heaven—but, more important, to offer them as role models. Those of us who are still trying to work out our salvation can try to emulate some of the virtues displayed by those who were so close to God that they were recognized for their holiness.

There are many more saints than just those the Church has officially canonized. To be a saint means simply that that person is in heaven where he or she is sharing forever a life that is divine and free from all decay. Naturally, we hope that all of us will be saints after we die, although there's not much chance that the Church will officially declare us so.

Certainly I believe, for example, that my mother and father are saints, enjoying the Beatific Vision in heaven.

There are various classifications of saints. The Blessed Virgin Mary is in a classification by herself since she is the mother of God. Next by way of honor are the Apostles, first the eleven men who followed Jesus (excluding Judas, who betrayed him) and then Matthias, who replaced Judas. Saint Paul and Saint Barnabas are also included as Apostles because of their importance in the early Church.

Next in honor are the martyrs, those who died rather than deny Christ. There have been martyrs in nearly every century, probably none more than during the twentieth century. Next are pastors, and these include especially holy popes, bishops, priests, abbots and missionaries. These are followed by the thirty-five Doctors of the Church. The word "doctor" comes from the Latin *docere*, which means to teach. These thirty-five people (thirty-one men and four women) are considered the Church's most accomplished teachers, whose combination of intellectual brilliance and sanctity has been of extraordinary importance in the development of doctrine or spirituality.

After the Doctors of the Church come virgins, women who never married and devoted their lives to serving the Church or people. Mother Teresa will fit in this category when she is canonized. Finally, we have the category of holy men and women, which covers those who don't fit into one of the other classifications. They could be men or women in religious orders, or those who worked with the underprivileged, or teachers. This is the category that married men and women are in.

One of the things some people object to regarding Catholics' devotion to the saints is the idea of praying for their intercession. That practice comes from the doctrine of the communion of saints that is part of the Apostles' Creed. Catholics believe that the saints in heaven—and that includes anyone in heaven, not just those who have been canonized—can pray for us, just as those on earth can do.

That brings us to the role of patron saints. These are saints who are acknowledged to be special protectors and intercessors for persons or churches. When we are baptized, we are encouraged to take, or be given in the case of a child, the name of a saint who will be our personal patron saint.

CHAPTER 25

EFFICACY OF PRAYER

What good does it do for us to pray? If we believe that God knows what is going to happen in the future, are our prayers going to make him change his mind? Furthermore, if God knows what we are going to do tomorrow, how can we say that we act freely?

These are questions that people have asked for centuries. It's hard to reconcile belief in the efficacy of prayer with God's omniscience.

It has helped me to reconcile those two concepts by trying to grasp another difficult concept—eternity. That, too, is hard for us humans, with our finite minds, to understand since it means the absence of time. For us, things happen moment after moment. What happened yesterday, or just a second ago, is past, and what will happen tomorrow, or the next year, is still in the future. But in eternity, there is no past and future. Everything will be simultaneous, in the present.

Of all the things I've read about the concept of eternity, perhaps nobody explained it any better than C. S. Lewis. This is his description of eternity, from a chapter titled "Time and Beyond Time" in his masterpiece *Mere Christianity*: "If you picture time as a straight line along which we have to travel, then you must picture God as the whole page on which the line is drawn. We come to the parts of the line one by one: we have to leave A behind before we get to B, and cannot reach C until we leave B behind. God, from above or outside or all around, contains the whole line, and sees it all."

This is important if we are to consider the question of human freedom despite the fact that God knows everything that is going to happen. God does not *foresee* us doing something tomorrow or next year anymore than he *saw* us doing something yesterday. He simply *sees* us doing it, whether past, present or future. In God's eternity both yesterday and tomorrow are eternally present. For you and me, yesterday is past and tomorrow hasn't come yet, but that's not true in eternity.

So God doesn't have to change his mind in order to answer our prayers and make something happen in our future that otherwise wouldn't have, because our future is the present for him. Furthermore, his knowledge of what we are going to do in the future doesn't destroy our freedom to decide whether or not we are going to do them. He knows our future actions to be the freely performed actions they are.

Other people have a different objection to prayer: How, they ask, could God possibly answer the prayers of all those people who are praying to him at the same time? Perhaps they visualize God handling one person's request and then moving on to another's and on down the line until everybody is taken care of. How, they ask, could he have time to handle all those requests?

Of course, that question itself involves "time" and God is not in time. He's in eternity. I suppose we could say that he has all the time he needs except that that answer contains the concept of time. Let's say that he has all eternity in which to listen to all those prayers.

It's well for us to become familiar with the concept of eternity since that's what we will experience after our death—a "time" without time. For me, at least, it also helps answer questions about the efficacy of prayer.

It also helps, by the way, to answer the question of how long someone has to remain in the process of purification we call purgatory. Those in purgatory are in eternity, where the concept of time is meaningless.

CHAPTER 26

DO I HAVE TO GO TO MASS?

You've probably heard it, perhaps even said it: "I don't have to go to Mass every Sunday to be a good Catholic." Or perhaps it's more along the lines of, "I have a close relationship with God, pray privately, and try to do good for others; I just don't get anything out of going to Mass."

A strange phenomenon is happening today. While more Catholics claim to be interested in spirituality, the number of those who regularly go to Mass keeps declining. Spirituality has become a private matter, divorced from the institutional Church. "I can pray in the quiet of my home; I don't have to go to church" has become a common refrain.

Perhaps this comes from the individualism that is often seen as an American virtue. We value individualism so much that we think of spirituality in strictly private terms.

Certainly private devotions, including periods of meditation or contemplation and the reading of Scripture, are to be encouraged. But one cannot be a true Catholic only privately. Catholicism has always been, and is meant to be, a communal religion.

Not only Catholicism. Judaism, too, is oriented to the community rather than to the individual. For example, the Jewish *Kaddish* (a memorial prayer for the dead) may be recited only if a *minyan* (a minimum prayer quorum) is present. And the *Viddui* which is recited on Yom Kippur stresses, "*We* have been guilty, *we* have betrayed, *we* have robbed."

When Jesus taught his disciples the Lord's Prayer, he prayed "*Our* Father," not "*My* Father," and he asked God to "give *us* our daily bread," "forgive *us* our trespasses," "lead *us* not into temptation," and "deliver *us* from evil." Even when we pray that prayer in private we are uniting ourselves with other Christians.

Catholic prayers directed to Mary, the mother of Jesus, follow that example. In the Hail Mary, we ask her to "pray for *us* sinners" and in the Hail Holy Queen (*Salve Regina*) plural nouns and pronouns are used throughout.

To understand why it's essential for good Catholics to attend Mass, whether or not they "get anything out of it," let's reflect on what a Catholic community is: It is the people of God gathered around the person of Christ and sharing in his Spirit. The Church is the people. It has Christ as its head, the Holy Spirit as the condition of its unity, the law of love as its rule, and the kingdom of God as its destiny.

All of us need some quiet time alone to develop our individual spirituality, but that must not replace joining others for worship. We humans are essentially social by nature and going to Mass is what we Catholics should do precisely so as not to be alone.

There are two great commandments, not one. The greatest is to love God, which we can do privately and individually, but the second is to love your neighbor as yourself, and it cannot be done without other people being involved. One of the reasons for going to church is to pray for and with some of those other people.

Saint Paul taught in his letters to the Romans, Corinthians, Ephesians and Colossians that we Christians are the Body of Christ. The body is not complete if some of its members are missing from the community.

There is a time and a place for private prayers and a time and place for communal prayers. We must stop trying to figure out what we can get out of going to Mass and concentrate more on what we can contribute by our presence and active participation in worshiping God. The purpose of going to Mass is to give adoration and praise to God—to give, not to receive. If we do that, we probably will quickly learn that we are also getting more out of going to Mass.

CHAPTER 27

LITURGY AND THE EUCHARIST

Saint Francis de Sales wrote in his *Introduction to the Devout Life*, "There is always more benefit and consolation to be derived from the public offices of the Church than from private particular acts. God has ordained that communion in prayer must always be preferred to every form of private prayer."

The public worship and acts of the Church are what we call its liturgy. It's the People of God participating together in the work of God. It's found mainly in the Eucharistic sacrifice (the Mass) and the sacraments.

Many men and women converts to Catholicism were first attracted to the Church by its liturgy. They found it more meaningful or more devout than what they found in other churches. That's because our liturgy includes scriptural readings, homilies, rituals, flowers, candles, vestments, incense, choirs, and many other things.

Despite these attractions, attendance at weekly Mass has slipped badly during recent decades because some Catholics simply have never learned to appreciate what we have in the Mass. It's both a sacrifice and a sacred meal. As a sacrifice, it's the memorial of Christ's work of salvation accomplished by his death and resurrection. We believe that it is Christ himself, through the priest celebrating the Mass, who offers the Eucharistic sacrifice and Christ himself, really present in the bread and wine, who is offered. The Church believes that the sacrifice of Christ on the cross and the sacrifice of the Eucharist are one single sacrifice. The same Christ who offered himself in a bloody manner on the cross offers himself in an unbloody manner on the altar.

As a sacred meal, we believe that we receive the body and blood of Jesus, really present under the appearance of bread and wine. When Jesus said, "This is my body" and "This is my blood" during the Last Supper, he meant what he said. Catholics call the change of bread and wine into Christ's body and blood "transubstantiation." It means that the *substance* of the bread and wine is changed while the appearances (color, composition, shape, taste) remain the same.

Thus there's a basic difference between what Catholics believe about the Eucharist and what most Protestants believe. Catholics believe that, when bread and wine are consecrated by a validly ordained Catholic priest, they really and truly become the body and blood of Jesus Christ. Although they continue to look and taste like bread and wine, the Council of Trent taught, "the body and blood, together with the soul and divinity, of our Lord Jesus Christ and, therefore, the whole Christ is truly, really, and substantially contained."

Admittedly, it takes a lot of faith to believe that. The great thirteenth century theologian Saint Thomas Aquinas said, "That in this sacrament are the true body of Christ and his true blood is something that cannot be apprehended by the senses, but only by faith, which relies on divine authority."

The "divine authority" he spoke of includes the statements of Jesus, found mainly in the sixth chapter of John's Gospel, verses 32 to 69. This is where he taught, "I am the bread of life" and, "Whoever eats my flesh and drinks my blood has eternal life." He repeated similar statements several times in this passage.

When some of his disciples decided that "this saying is hard; who can accept it?" and, "as a result of this, many of his disciples returned to their former way of life and no longer accompanied him," Jesus did not back off. He meant what he said.

That, then, is the rationale behind the Catholic Church's belief in what it calls the real presence of Christ in the Eucharist. Furthermore, the Catholic Church teaches that Jesus instituted the Eucharistic sacrifice of his body and blood at the Last Supper in order to perpetuate the sacrifice of the cross throughout the ages.

This belief is so strong in the Catholic Church that the *Catechism of the Catholic Church* says, "The Eucharist is the sum and summary of our faith" (No. 1327) and, "The Eucharist is the source and summit of the Christian life" (No. 1324).

CHAPTER 28

OTHER SACRAMENTS

Besides the Eucharist, the Catholic Church has six other sacraments. Sacraments, by the way, are defined as "efficacious signs of grace, instituted by Christ and entrusted to the Church, by which divine life is dispensed to us" (*Catechism of the Catholic Church*, No. 1131).

By "efficacious signs," we mean that they are effective. They're effective because Christ is at work in them. Each of the sacraments brings some particular grace special to that sacrament. We believe that Christ himself instituted every one of the sacraments at some point during his life and gave them to the Church that he founded. Finally, through the sacraments, we receive divine life, or holiness.

The Church groups the seven sacraments into three categories. Baptism, Confirmation, and the Eucharist are called the sacraments of initiation. Penance and Reconciliation, and Anointing of the Sick are considered sacraments of healing. Holy Orders and Matrimony are sacraments at the service of communion.

We believe that Baptism is necessary for salvation because Jesus told Nicodemus, "No one can enter the Kingdom of God without being born of water and Spirit" (John 3:5). There was a time when babies were baptized shortly after their birth because of high infant mortality. The Church still wants those babies to be baptized early, but not before parents are properly prepared to raise them as Catholics.

Confirmation is another sacrament of initiation, this time usually for children in their early teens. Adults, though, are also frequently confirmed, especially those who enter the Church on Holy Saturday. This sacrament is sometimes called the sacrament of the Holy Spirit because the third person of the Trinity comes upon the person to strengthen him or her for an adult service to the Church. A bishop ordinarily administers this sacrament, especially to children, but bishops usually entrust priests to do so in the case of adults who are being baptized or admitted to full communion with the Church. We believe that Christ instituted this sacrament on the night of his resurrection when he breathed on the Apostles and said, "Receive the Holy Spirit" (John 20:22).

Jesus instituted the sacrament of Penance and Reconciliation during this same appearance to the Apostles when he said, "Whose sins you forgive are forgiven them, and whose sins you retain are retained" (John 20:23). This sacrament requires contrition on the part of the sinner, confession to a priest, absolution by the priest in the name of Jesus, and an act of penance as a way to make satisfaction of the sins confessed.

The Gospels tell us about many occasions when Jesus healed the sick, and the Church continues his ministry of healing through the sacrament of the Anointing of the Sick. In this sacrament, it is Jesus himself, through the priest, who touches the sick to heal them from their sins and perhaps also from a physical ailment. The primary effect is spiritual healing, the sick person's sins forgiven if he or she is unable to confess his or her sins in the sacrament of Penance and Reconciliation.

I should mention that this sacrament was once called Extreme Unction, or the Last Rites, and was administered to someone who was dying. That is no longer the case. Today the Church's Last Rites include three sacraments: Penance, Anointing of the Sick, and the Eucharist as *Viaticum*, or food for the journey.

Holy Orders is the name given to the sacrament that ordains men for service to the Church. The word "order" came from the Roman Empire, where it referred to a governing group, and there are three "orders" of ordination—bishops, priests and deacons. The *Catechism of the Catholic Church* says that ordination "confers a gift of the Holy Spirit that permits the exercise of a 'sacred power' . . . which can come only from Christ himself through the Church" (No. 1538).

I'll discuss the sacrament of Matrimony in the next chapter.

CHAPTER 29

MARRIAGE IN GOD'S PLAN

It's impossible to pretend that marriage is a thriving institution in the United States. The numbers of couples who live together without marriage, the divorce rate, and the numbers of children born outside of marriage, continue to skyrocket. The concept of "marriage" between two people of the same sex is gaining ever wider acceptance.

If we can do little more than bemoan these facts, we can at least present a positive picture of marriage in God's plan because we are convinced that it offers men and women the best chance at happiness in their lives.

The Church teaches us that God himself is the author of marriage. In Genesis we read that, in marriage, "a man leaves his father and his mother and cleaves to his wife, and they become one flesh" (2:24). Jesus confirmed that when he said that husband and wife "are no longer two, but one flesh" (Matthew 19:6).

This means, in plain English, that these two people are a single organism. As C. S. Lewis wrote in *Mere Christianity*, "The inventor of the human machine was telling us that its two halves, the male and the female, were made to be combined together in pairs, not simply on the sexual level, but totally combined." That is why, as Jesus said, "What God has joined together, no human being must separate" (Matthew 19:7).

We Catholics believe that Jesus raised the human institution of marriage to the dignity of one of the seven sacraments. By his presence at the wedding at Cana, Jesus confirmed the goodness of marriage and proclaimed that from then on marriage would be an efficacious sign of his presence. Through this sacrament, spouses are strengthened and consecrated for the duties and the dignity of marriage.

When they marry, husbands and wives establish a matrimonial covenant, a partnership between themselves, that by its very nature is ordered toward the good of the spouses as well as toward the procreation and education of their children—what the Church considers to be the two major purposes of marriage. Try as it might, secular society can find nothing else that better serves those purposes.

That is why the Church insists that a marriage covenant—between a baptized man and a baptized woman, both free to contract marriage, who freely express their consent—cannot be dissolved once the marriage has been consummated through sexual intercourse. The consent of the marriage partners to give and receive each other is a bond sealed by God himself, and it cannot be broken.

Needless to say, our modern society doesn't accept God's plan for marriage. "Being in love" seems to be the only reason for getting married or remaining married, and that leaves no room for marriage as a covenant or a permanent bond. The strange thing is, as G. K. Chesterton once pointed out, couples who are deeply in love have a natural inclination to bind themselves by promises.

It should go without saying that marriage in God's plan requires fidelity of both spouses. Not only is this essential to preserve the covenant, but, as the *Catechism of the Catholic Church* says, "The deepest reason is found in the fidelity of God to his covenant, in that of Christ to his Church. Through the sacrament of matrimony the spouses are enabled to represent this fidelity and witness to it" (No. 1647).

Marriage is indeed part of God's plan, not only a social construct. As the *Catechism of the Catholic Church* says, "The vocation to marriage is written in the very nature of man and woman as they came from the hand of the Creator. Marriage is not a purely human institution despite the many variations it may have undergone through the centuries in different cultures, social structures and spiritual attitudes" (No. 1603).

Despite what modern society might teach, this is the meaning of marriage in God's plan. Cohabitation, single motherhood, or any other modern substitutes for marriage simply can't match God's plan. We can count on the Church to continue to emphasize the importance of marriage despite our society's efforts to minimize it.

CHAPTER 30

THE ROSARY

The rosary is usually associated with Catholics, although people of other faiths sometimes also pray this devotion. It has been called the perfect Christian prayer because it combines prayer, meditation and Scripture. The repetition of prayers is meant to create an atmosphere in which to meditate on the mysteries of our salvation as revealed in Scripture.

Although the prayer said most often with the rosary is the Hail Mary, addressed to Jesus' mother, the main focus is on the birth, life, death and resurrection of Jesus. These are the "mysteries" or events that the pray-er thinks about while praying the rosary.

The rosary consists of a string of beads divided into five sets known as decades because they have ten beads in each set. Besides ten smaller beads, each set has one large bead. While meditating, the person prays a Hail Mary on each smaller bead and the Our Father on the large beads. Sometimes those praying the rosary will add a few additional prayers, but five Our Fathers and fifty Hail Marys basically make up the rosary.

The Our Father and Hail Mary are scriptural prayers. Jesus himself taught his Apostles the Our Father (Matthew 6:9-13, Luke 11:2-4). The Hail Mary includes Gabriel's greeting to Mary, "Hail, full of grace, the Lord is with thee" (Luke 1:28) and Elizabeth's exclamation, "Blessed art thou among women and blessed is the fruit of thy womb" (Luke 1:42). The prayer than concludes with the petition, "Holy Mary, mother of God, pray for us sinners now and at the hour of our death. Amen."

The rosary was begun in the late twelfth century when laity began to pray one hundred fifty Hail Marys in imitation of the one hundred fifty psalms. Saint Dominic and his followers popularized it in the thirteenth century, adding the meditations about the life of Jesus.

In the early fifteenth century, the Carthusian monk Dominic of Prussia divided the one hundred fifty Hail Marys into three sets of fifty. He also began to call each of the fifty points of meditation a *rosarium* (rose garden) because the rose was a symbol of joy and Mary was "the cause of our joy" for bearing Christ. Thus the name "rosary" became the name for the devotion.

Another fifteenth-century Carthusian monk, Henry of Kalkar, then divided the fifty Hail Marys into decades with an Our Father between each. In 1483 a Dominican priest wrote a book on the rosary called *Our Dear Lady's Psalter*. It listed the same fifteen mysteries that we meditated about through the twentieth century except that the fourth glorious mystery combined Mary's assumption and coronation and the fifth glorious mystery was the Last Judgment.

For more than five hundred years there were fifteen official mysteries: five joyful, which concern the beginning of our redemption (the Annunciation, the Visitation, the Nativity, the presentation in the Temple, and finding the child Jesus in the Temple); five sorrowful, which pertain to Christ's passion (the agony in the garden, the scourging, the crowning with thorns, the carrying of the cross, and the crucifixion); and the glorious (the Resurrection, the Ascension, the descent of the Holy Spirit, the Assumption and the Coronation of Mary).

There was an obvious gap between the finding of Jesus in the Temple when he was twelve and his passion and death. Therefore, in 2002 Blessed John Paul II added the five luminous mysteries, or mysteries of light, recalling events in Jesus' public ministry—his baptism, the wedding feast at Cana, the proclamation of the Kingdom of God, the Transfiguration, and the institution of the Eucharist. With those additions, the rosary really is what Pope Paul VI called it in his 1974 apostolic exhortation *Marialis Cultus*: "a compendium of the entire Gospel."

Some people pray what is called the Scriptural Rosary. It includes a Scripture text to be read before each Hail Mary.

From all reports, many Catholics have returned to the practice of saying the rosary daily after some decades of this devotion fading in its popularity. It never should have faded since the rosary had been an important part of Catholicism for about eight centuries.

CHAPTER 31

VENERATION OF STATUES

While I was writing a monthly column about Catholicism for the daily newspaper *The Indianapolis Star*, I naturally received many questions from readers. One of them was: "Why do you people worship statues when the Second Commandment forbids making graven images?" By "you people" the questioner meant Catholics.

The role of statues is one of the things asked most frequently about Catholicism. (Others are Catholics' belief in the real presence of Jesus in the Eucharist, the reason for devotion to Jesus' mother Mary, and belief in purgatory.)

Before answering the question, I first have to point out that Christians of other denominations number the Ten Commandments differently and that Catholics include the prohibition against making graven images as part of the First Commandment.

The short answer to why Catholics worship statues is: we don't. Religious worship is not directed to images in themselves, considered as mere things, but to that which they represent—God, Mary, or other saints. But that answer is hardly satisfactory.

Controversies about the veneration of images aren't new. They were especially prominent in the eighth and ninth centuries in the Eastern Church. There, though, they involved icons (or ikons), which are representations of Jesus, Mary or a saint painted on a wall, a partition or a wooden panel. The icons of the Eastern Churches take the place of the statues of the West.

In the eighth century Byzantine Emperor Leo III became convinced that icons fostered idolatry and that they were prohibited by the biblical ban on graven images. Therefore, in 726 Leo issued an edict in which he declared that all images, icons included, were idolatrous and he ordered them to be destroyed. This began what was called the Iconoclastic Controversy from a Greek word meaning "image-breaking."

Leo's edict immediately met bitter opposition, especially from the Eastern Church's monks, who had long taught the fine art of painting icons. John of Damascus wrote a spirited defense of the veneration of icons, saying, "What the written word is to those who know letters the icon is to the unlettered; what speech is to the ear, the icon is to the eye." Pope Gregory III condemned iconoclasm in 731.

The Eastern emperors, though, continued their iconoclastic policies for more than fifty years, until Empress Irene ruled as regent for her son, Constantine V. Irene believed in icons so she and Patriarch Tarasius of Constantinople wrote to Pope Adrian I asking for a council to resolve the Iconoclastic Controversy. The seventh ecumenical council, known as the Second Council of Nicaea, opened on September 27, 787.

The council promulgated a decree that approved the setting up of images but said that they were not to be worshiped since the act of worship belongs only to God. It distinguished between the worship that is due to God and the "relative honor" that is given to icons. It quoted Saint Basil as saying that the honor paid to sacred images is a "respectful veneration" and "whoever venerates an image venerates the person portrayed in it."

But that begs the question, "Are we permitted to venerate Mary and other saints?" Invocation of and devotion to the saints are as ancient as Christianity itself and are based on Saint Paul's doctrine of the Mystical Body of Christ expressed in several of his letters. The earliest expression of such veneration was shown by reverence given to the martyrs.

Through the centuries Christians have prayed to the saints asking their intercession with God on our behalf. As I've pointed out in previous chapters, this is part of the communion of saints that we say we believe in when we recite the Apostles' Creed. We believe that a spiritual communion exists among the saints in heaven, the souls of the dead still undergoing purification, and those of us still living on earth.

The icons of the Eastern Churches and the paintings and statues of the Western Church keep God and his saints before our minds and hearts just as old photos of our parents or grandparents do.

CHAPTER 32

WHY ARE WE HERE?

It is part of human nature to consider the ultimate questions about the meaning and purpose of life. Even the most primitive cultures have done so, with varying answers.

Some of the answers have come down to us in the Jewish scriptures Christians know as the Old Testament, perhaps especially in the Book of Ecclesiastes and the Book of Proverbs. The conclusion of the Book of Proverbs is that "all things are vanity." The author examines the things that humans usually search for—wisdom, pleasure, riches, renown—and find them all lacking, "a chase after wind."

The Book of Proverbs is considerably more optimistic than the Book of Ecclesiastes. Of all the Wisdom Books, it is probably the one that best provides the guide for successful living that the ancient Israelites sought.

What about people today? In the midst of our busy lives, spent in the most prosperous nation in history, do we take time out to reflect on why we are here? Certainly the secular society in which we live doesn't encourage such reflection. It encourages us rather to keep pushing ourselves to succeed in business, to buy as many of the luxuries our economy produces as we can, to enjoy our entertainments. But why?

Secular society doesn't have the answer to that question? Religion does. It's up to our religious leaders to remind us that there is an ultimate purpose to our lives.

For me, as a Catholic of a certain age, I have always felt comfortable with the answer to the question "Why did God make you?" that I learned as a child: *God made me to know him, to love him, and to serve him in this life and to be happy with him forever in the next.* I have heard and read many more sophisticated philosophies of the meaning of life but they all seem to boil down to that rather simple answer.

But that simple answer implies considerable work on our part. First we must come to know God, which means studying as much about him as he has deemed fit to reveal to us. Once we know God we can't help but love him since, as the First Letter of John tells us, "God is love." And if we truly love God, we will want to serve him. To do that means first and foremost to discover in our daily lives God's unique vocations for us. I think we all have many vocations—many calls from God. All of us are called, above all, to obey the two great commandments: first, you shall love the Lord your God with all your heart, with all your being, with all your strength, and with all your mind; and, second, you shall love your neighbor as yourself.

Then God calls us to specific ways to do that at different stages of our lives. We all have calls from God to use the unique gifts and talents he has given us to accomplish his will for us. We receive many calls as we proceed through life and we must never stop trying to discern what God is calling us to do—*now*. God's call might be different when we are in our forties, sixties, or eighties than when we were in our twenties.

Therefore, we have multiple vocations. God calls us to serve society and the Church by using our unique talents, whatever they might be. When we choose our profession, surely God isn't calling us to pick something only because it will enable us to earn the most money. Our calling is to use God's gifts for the benefit of others.

It's in discerning God's will for us that we discover why we are here.

CHAPTER 33

OUR MULTIPLE VOCATIONS

I said in the previous chapter that, if we are to know, love and serve God, we must do that by discerning our vocations—our calls—from God.

Father Henri Nouwen, the prolific and best-selling author who died in 1996, distinguished between vocation and career in his book *Creative Ministry*. "A career disconnected from a vocation divides," he wrote. "A career that expresses obedience to our vocation is the concrete way of making our unique talents available to the community."

We receive many calls from God to make "our unique talents available to the community" and our jobs should usually be seen as at least one of those vocations. We are expected to glorify God by our work. We can and should offer our work to God and achieve our salvation through our work.

All honest and moral work has equal value if it is done well, whether it is work in the home, as a waitress or dishwasher, a factory worker, a lawyer or businessman, a politician, or even a journalist. There should be no distinction between "prestigious" and "modest" work. But to have spiritual value, work must be done well. The work that is best from a spiritual viewpoint is ordinary work done extraordinarily well.

Labor is an essential part of God's plan for humans. In the Book of Genesis we read that "the Lord God then took the man and settled him in the garden of Eden, to cultivate and care for it" (2:15). Jesus himself sanctified work by spending most of his life as an obscure carpenter in Galilee. And Saint Paul prided himself on his work as a tentmaker while preaching about Jesus.

We would do well, though, to remember that our job is not an end in itself. The ultimate goal, in our work as in everything else we do, is the glorification of God. This can be done even through boring and routine work, especially when it is done as a means of supporting a family. Or it can be done by working as a volunteer, doing work for which there is no payment.

Or perhaps the job itself is not a calling, but only the opportunity it provides for our true vocation—that of witnessing to our faith through our relations with those we meet in our daily work.

The early part of our careers usually corresponds to the early years of our marriages and the raising of our families, and our vocation is to do that to the best of our abilities and energy. As we age, though, surely the opportunities we have for volunteer services should be seen as God's call. Such opportunities seem endless in both society and in our parishes.

We need good men and women to serve in governmental positions, either elected or appointed, and God calls some of us to do that. He calls others to serve in the military or as police officers or firemen. He calls others to serve the poor by volunteering for work with the Saint Vincent de Paul Society. He calls volunteers in our parishes to be lectors, extraordinary ministers of Holy Communion, ushers, choir members, collection counters, members of school commissions or parish councils, or religious education teachers. Some men are called to be permanent deacons.

Our society has come to accept what we call second vocations, changes in professions during middle age. Many men and women have recognized their vocations to the priesthood or religious life after years spent in secular occupations. Does that mean that they missed their vocations earlier in life? Probably not. In all likelihood, they were following God's call both times because he continually calls us to serve him and others in different ways.

Mother Teresa once told me and some other journalists I was with: "You cannot do what I do, but I cannot do what you do. Each of us has his or her own work to do. The important thing is that we do something beautiful for God." How could it be expressed better than that?

CHAPTER 34

THE NATURAL LAW AND
THE TEN COMMANDMENTS

Pope Emeritus Benedict spoke frequently about the natural law.

What is the natural law? Saint Paul expressed it most simply when he wrote to the Romans that even those who have not heard of the law of Moses, the Ten Commandments, still know what is right and wrong because "what the law requires is written on their hearts" (Romans 2:15). Pope Benedict XVI repeated Saint Paul's definition in his 2008 New Year's address when he explained natural law as "written on the heart of the human being and made known to him by reason."

It's the standard by which human beings know, by the use of their reason, what actions are right and what actions are wrong. The *Catechism of the Catholic Church* says, "The natural law expresses the original moral sense which enables man to discern by reason the good and the evil, the truth and the lie" (No. 1954).

The *United States Catholic Catechism for Adults* adds, "Through our human reason, we can come to understand the true purpose of the created order. The natural law is thus our rational appreciation of the divine plan. It expresses our human dignity and is the foundation of our basic human rights and duties. This law within us leads us to choose the good that it reveals" (Pg. 327).

When C. S. Lewis was putting together broadcasts that eventually became *Mere Christianity*, he began with a discussion of right and wrong. His first broadcast, and later first chapter in the book, was titled "The Law of Human Nature." He said, "This law was called the Law of Nature because people thought that everyone knew it by nature and did not need to be taught it."

He pointed out that, although civilizations sometimes had different moralities, "these have never amounted to anything like a total difference. If anyone will take the trouble to compare the moral teaching of, say, the ancient Egyptians, Babylonians, Hindus, Chinese, Greeks and Romans, what will really strike him will be how very like they are to each other and to our own."

It's true that some of those civilizations practiced human sacrifice to their gods, which seems contrary to natural law (as do suicide bombings today), but generally all societies have condemned murder, adultery, robbery, and injustices of all types.

To be clear, we cannot rely solely on the natural law when it comes to doctrines of our faith. We cannot reason our way to the truths of our faith that have been revealed by God—the Trinity, Incarnation and Redemption, for example, or belief in Jesus' presence in the Eucharist. The natural law applies to morality rather than to revealed doctrine.

God's plan for humans' morality was revealed in the Old Testament by the Ten Commandments that he gave to Moses. The *Catechism of the Catholic Church* describes the Ten Commandments as "the privileged expression of the natural law" (No. 2070) because we believe that the prohibitions in the Commandments, as well as such positive Commandments as "Honor your father and your mother," are clearly also part of the natural law.

The Ten Commandments, though, are more than part of the natural law. They are also laws that God has revealed to us. They begin with three Commandments that treat our relationship to God: "I, the Lord, am your God . . . . You shall not have other gods besides me," "You shall not take the name of the Lord your God in vain," and "Remember to keep holy the Lord's day."

The other seven treat of our relationship with each other: "Honor your father and your mother," "You shall not kill," "You shall not commit adultery," "You shall not steal," "You shall not bear false witness against your neighbor," "You shall not covet your neighbor's wife," and "You shall not covet your neighbor's goods."

We Catholics believe that the Old Law prepared the world for the Gospel of the New Testament. Revelation in Jesus fulfills the natural law and God's plan as revealed in the Old Testament.

CHAPTER 35

ABSOLUTE MORAL NORMS

"What is truth?"

That, of course, is the question Pontius Pilate asked Jesus when Jesus said that he had come into the world to testify to the truth. It appears, though, that Pilate isn't the only one who was confused about what truth is. Apparently so are most Americans. A survey conducted in 2002 discovered that most Americans believe moral truth "always depends upon the situation" and they reject the idea of unchanging "moral absolutes." According to the poll results, this is true of the majority of people in all age categories.

A whopping eighty-three percent of teens said that moral truth always depends on the situation or circumstance. Young adults who believe that weren't far behind—seventy-five percent. It was fifty-five percent for those aged thirty-six to fifty-five and sixty-one percent for those over fifty-five. These people all seem to believe in relativism.

When asked how they base their ethical or moral choices, only twenty percent of teens said they did so on "principles or standards." The most common answer, thirty-three percent, was "whatever feels right or comfortable."

Contrary to what all these people think, there *are* moral absolutes. There *is* objective truth and it doesn't depend upon the situation.

Although we should be saddened by the results of those polls, we really shouldn't be surprised. As far back as 1993, Pope John Paul II noted what he called "a crisis of truth." To try to combat that crisis, he wrote his encyclical *Veritatis Splendor* ("The Splendor of Truth").

He showed that he understood the attitude of the majority of those polled when he wrote, "In contemporary moral thinking all discussions are closely related to one crucial issue: 'human freedom.' Today people have a strong sense of freedom, due to a heightened sense of the dignity of the human person and of his or her uniqueness. This is definitely a positive achievement of modern culture, but it is expressed sometimes in ways that diverge from the truth about the human person as a creature in the image of God, ways that need to be corrected and purified in the light of faith."

Later in that encyclical he wrote, "Human persons are free. But their freedom is not unlimited; it must halt before the moral law given by God. Human freedom finds its fulfillment precisely in the acceptance of that law. God's law does not reduce or do away with human freedom; instead it protects and promotes that freedom."

We'd like to put a positive spin on the response of those surveyed who said they do "whatever feels right and comfortable." Perhaps, if given the choice, they would have said, "I follow my conscience." Saint Bonaventure taught us, "Conscience is like God's herald and messenger. This is why conscience has binding force."

Saint Paul taught the Romans, "They [the Gentiles] show that the demands of the law are written in their hearts, while their conscience also bears witness and their conflicting thoughts accuse or even defend them" (Romans 2:15).

Pope John Paul echoed Saint Paul: "Conscience is the application of the natural law to a particular case, an inner dictate for the individual, a summons to do what is good in a particular situation, respecting the universality of the law" (No. 59). I hope this is what the people meant when they said they would choose whatever feels right and comfortable in a given situation. If they have a rightly formed conscience and they follow it, they will feel right and comfortable.

Some acts, however, are intrinsically evil. In *Gaudium et Spes*, the Second Vatican Council listed a number of such acts, especially "whatever is hostile to life itself" (No. 27). And the *Catechism of the Catholic Church* teaches, "There are certain specific kinds of behavior that are always wrong to choose, because choosing them involves a disorder of the will, that is, a moral evil" (No. 1761).

Jesus said, "If you remain in my word, you will truly be my disciples, and you will know the truth, and the truth will set you free" (John 8:31-32).

CHAPTER 36

RELATIVISM AND CONSCIENCE

The day before he was elected Pope Benedict XVI, Cardinal Joseph Ratzinger spoke out against what he called a new "dictatorship of relativism" that has pervaded society. It was interesting to see the secular media try to define relativism, none very accurately.

Basically, relativism is the belief that there is no such thing as absolute truth, that truth is relative. What is true for you might not be true for me. We see the results of such a philosophy in our society's embrace of tolerance.

Harvey Cox taught Harvard undergraduates a course in "Jesus as a moral teacher" for about twenty years. In his book *When Jesus Came to Harvard*, Cox says that, in his discussions with his students, he soon learned that the virtue his students valued most was tolerance. They loathed being looked upon as judgmental.

They were, he said, "benevolent but uncomfortable relativists." However, he wrote, "I was glad they were coming to realize that a nation with two hundred fifty million separate moral codes is an impossibility, and a world with six billion individuals each doing his or her own thing would become unlivable."

Pope Benedict probably had long discussions about the falsity of relativism with his predecessor, Pope John Paul II, while Pope Benedict was head of the Congregation for the Doctrine of the Faith for twenty-four years. Pope John Paul condemned relativism often, including in his encyclical *Veritatis Splendor* ("The Splendor of Truth") that he issued in 1993 just after the publication of the *Catechism of the Catholic Church*. The third sentence of that encyclical said, "People are constantly tempted by Satan to exchange 'the truth about God for a lie' (Romans 1:25), giving themselves over to relativism and skepticism."

The encyclical called everyone to "act in accordance with the judgment of conscience." However, it said (as Pope John Paul also had said in his encyclical *Dominum et Vivificantem* ("Lord and Giver of Life"), "Conscience does not establish the law; it bears witness to the authority of the natural law" and, "In order to have a 'good conscience' one must seek the truth and make one's judgments accordingly" (No. 60).

The catechism, by the way, devotes twenty-seven paragraphs (1776-1802) to the conscience, including the formation of conscience, which, it says, "is a lifelong task."

Unfortunately, too many people today have a mistaken idea of the role of conscience. It has come to mean the freedom to act as one thinks best, each person choosing his or her own ideas of morality: "If it feels good to me it must be OK." This is almost synonymous with relativism.

Pope Francis includes an entire section of his first encyclical, *Lumen Fidei* ("The Light of Faith") to the relationship between faith and truth. He decries the fact that, in contemporary culture, "we are willing to allow for subjective truths of the individual, which consist in fidelity to his or her deepest convictions, yet these are truths valid only for that individual and not capable of being proposed to others in an effort to serve the common good. Yet Truth itself, the truth which would comprehensively explain our life as individuals and in society, is regarded with suspicion. In the end, what we are left with is relativism, in which the question of universal truth—and ultimately this means the question of God—is no longer relevant."

Cardinal John Henry Newman wrote often about the role of conscience. For him, conscience meant much more than a person's preference or the right to reject a teaching of the Church. In his *Letter to the Duke of Norfolk*, he wrote, "Conscience is not a long-sighted selfishness, nor a desire to be consistent with oneself; but it is a messenger from him who, both in nature and grace, speaks to us behind a veil, and teaches and rules us by his representatives."

A well-formed conscience is difficult to achieve. If we find ourselves at odds with the Church over some matter, our obligation is not to reject the teaching but rather to form our consciences in conformity with the Church as the most reliable authority on matters of faith and morals.

CHAPTER 37

SPIRITUAL AND RELIGIOUS

You have probably seen, or perhaps heard, someone comment that he or she "is spiritual but not religious." It seems to be an excuse for seeking spiritual experiences while steadfastly avoiding any type of organized religion.

Americans seem always to be seeking the spiritual. Bookstores are full of books that tell how to harness our spiritual energy or "find our true selves." Experts lead us away from harmful addictions and help us to find inner peace through meditation. New Age spirituality has undoubtedly become popular as people are searching for spiritual values in our secular society.

But many of these people absolutely reject religion like a plague. They see spirituality as freedom but religion as confining. They want to experience the magnificence of a sunrise rather than sit in a dreary church listening to a boring preacher.

These people don't realize that spirituality without religion is incomplete. Obviously, there is nothing wrong with spirituality, but one can be both spiritual and religious. It's "both/and," not "either/or." A good Catholic uses the gifts that religion provides to make him or her more spiritual.

Too much of what passes for spirituality today is narcissistic. It smacks of a self-improvement system. It's geared toward making one feel better, either physically or mentally. That's fine as far as it goes, but it doesn't go far enough.

Religion reaches out to others—or at least it should. It teaches love of God and love of neighbor because of our love for God. It's possible to have spiritual experiences that have no relationship with God, but they are incomplete.

Saint Thomas Aquinas said that religion is that part of the virtue of justice in which we human beings publicly and privately give God the worship due to him. It means observing what Jesus called the greatest commandment: "You shall love the Lord your God with all your heart, and with all your soul and with all your strength" (Deuteronomy 6:5).

When we do that, we combine spirituality with religion. We become both spiritual and religious. Then we should carry it a bit further and accept Jesus Christ's call to unite with others in communion with his mystical body, the Church. Through the graces we receive in baptism and the other sacraments, we are connected deeply to Christ and to all others whom he has redeemed.

Spirituality is a deeply personal thing, different for every individual. Within Catholicism, however, we are offered all kinds of help to develop our spirituality. Catholicism has a vast body of writings about spirituality, beginning with Saint Paul and including Saints Augustine, Teresa of Avila, John of the Cross, Bernard, Thomas Aquinas, Ignatius of Loyola, Therese of Lisieux, and numerous others. In more modern times, we have books by Thomas Merton, Henri Nouwen, Basil Pennington and the Protestant author Kathleen Norris, among others.

The Church offers a variety of spiritualities, including Ignatian, Salesian, Franciscan, Carmelite and Benedictine. Religious orders offer oblate programs—members who are not solemnly professed but who try to live the charisms of the orders within their particular state in life.

Meditation and contemplative prayer have always been staples of Christian prayer. Today "centering prayer" (a form of contemplation) is being taught in many places. It is no longer confined to monasteries of men and women religious but is regularly being practiced by lay people as an important part of their spiritual life.

Within the Catholic Church there is some form of spirituality to satisfy anyone. There are charismatic groups for those who find that type of prayer appealing, or Taize prayer groups for those who are interested in that. The rosary is prayed in most parishes for the more traditional Catholics. Small Christian communities, faith sharing groups and Bible study groups are common.

Our churches are available for people to experience their spirituality before the Blessed Sacrament, either in those parishes where perpetual adoration is practiced or simply before the tabernacle.

The point is, the Catholic Church provides the opportunity for everyone to be both spiritual and religious. One does not have to choose one or the other.

CHAPTER 38

THE LIFE ISSUES

Catholics are—I insist that they must be—pro-life. Unfortunately, there are people who identify themselves as Catholics and call themselves pro-choice when it comes to abortion, but they have to know that they are in opposition to the teachings of the Church.

We believe that all human life is sacred because, as the *Catechism of the Catholic Church* says, "God alone is the Lord of life from its beginning until its end: no one can under any circumstance claim for himself the right directly to destroy an innocent human being" (No. 2258).

The label "pro-life" usually comes up over the issue of abortion and the Church has condemned abortion ever since the *Didache (The Teaching of the Apostles)* was written toward the end of the first century. It includes the commandment, "You shall not kill the embryo by abortion" (No. 2).

The admonition not to destroy an innocent human being doesn't mean only abortion, of course. At the other end of life, it means euthanasia, the killing of people who are sick, disabled, or dying. Even if it might seem to be merciful to put someone out of his or her misery, it is always wrong to take direct action to cause someone's death or to discontinue procedures that are keeping someone alive. However, the catechism instructs us, "Discontinuing medical procedures that are burdensome, dangerous, extraordinary, or disproportionate to the expected outcome can be legitimate; it is the refusal of 'over-zealous' treatment. Here one does not will to cause death; one's inability to impede it is merely accepted" (No. 2278). It's also legitimate to give patients heavy doses of narcotics to relieve pain even if those narcotics have the risk of hastening death.

There has been much talk in recent years about embryonic stem-cell research. The Church condemns any research on the human embryo that causes its death. Biology, not religious doctrine, tells us that human life begins at conception—when a human sperm fertilizes a human egg. After that happens, religious belief tells us that we may not kill it. No matter how much good scientists think they might be able to do by experimenting on embryos, the willful destruction of that embryo is the killing of human life. Every successful experiment so far has been done with adult stem cells anyway, which doesn't involve the killing of embryos.

Advocates of embryo experimentation like to point out that there are hundreds of thousands of frozen embryos that were produced by *in vitro* fertilization and there is no possibility that they will ever grow to become a viable baby. Nevertheless, to discard or kill those embryos is the taking of human life. Besides, the Church doesn't approve of *in vitro* fertilization, no matter how helpful it has been for couples who want a baby, because it separates procreation from the unitive act of sexual intercourse.

The Catholic Church also opposes capital punishment in most cases, although this prohibition is a bit different from other acts of killing because it doesn't involve the killing of an *innocent* human being. This teaching has evolved because the Church hasn't always opposed the death penalty. The Church still teaches that governmental authority has the right and duty to assure the safety of society, including the imposition of the death penalty if there is no other way to protect society. However, taking the lead of Pope John Paul II's encyclical *The Gospel of Life*, the teaching now is that non-lethal means are nearly always available to protect society from murderers. Therefore, capital punishment is not necessary. When it is carried out, it should not be for reasons of revenge. We don't kill someone to teach that it's wrong to kill someone.

The Catholic Church also opposes war, but it is not pacifist. It believes that there can be, and have been, just wars—especially defensive wars against countries or terrorists who threaten one's homeland. The *United States Catholic Catechism for Adults* says, "War may never be undertaken from a spirit of vengeance, but rather from motives of self-defense and of establishing justice and right order." Furthermore, from the time of Saint Augustine in the fifth century, the Church has laid down specific conditions for a war to be moral or just.

CHAPTER 39

ABORTION AND COMMUNION

I really hate to admit it, but the Catholic Church has not done a good job of convincing all Catholics either of the evil of abortion or the seriousness of receiving Communion only when one is in the state of grace. The evidence for that statement is the controversy that comes up whenever bishops tell political candidates that they may not receive Communion if they support abortion.

The problem of pro-abortion Catholic politicians receiving Holy Communion was a national issue when Democrat John Kerry was running for president in 2004. More recently it came up with Vice President Joe Biden and former Speaker of the House Congresswoman Nancy Pelosi, who are pro-choice. Catholics have an obligation to respect life, and it is a grievous sin to encourage abortion. Those with any grievous sin on their souls are not worthy to receive Communion.

This is not just a rule for politicians. It applies to everybody. It also isn't a matter of the Catholic bishops getting involved in partisan politics. They are defending what the Church has consistently taught about the Eucharist ever since Saint Paul warned the Corinthians that people may not receive Communion "unworthily," which it has defined as being in the state of mortal sin. It's a sacrilege to do so.

Any mortal sin—adultery, skipping Sunday Mass, stealing a large amount of money, defaming someone's good name, etc.—is incompatible with going to Communion. But the present controversy concerns abortion. Anyone who votes for a politician precisely because he or she supports abortion rights, while knowing that that is grievously wrong, is committing a mortal sin and may not receive Communion.

The U.S. bishops have not taken a united stand on the issue of whether priests should *refuse* Communion to pro-abortion politicians. There's agreement that such politicians should not present themselves for Communion but not on whether they should be refused if they do.

Meanwhile, we have to face the fact that the Church still has a serious need to educate the faithful about the seriousness of the issue of abortion. Those states with the highest percentage of Catholics are those with the most pro-abortion politicians—Massachusetts, for example. Or Rhode Island, which has the highest percentage of Catholics in the nation and where polls say that sixty-three percent of the people are pro-choice. As much as the popes and bishops have emphasized life issues, they apparently have not been able to convince most Catholics. And it's not just abortion, but also euthanasia, embryonic stem-cell research, and capital punishment, too.

The *Catechism of the Catholic Church* clearly teaches, "Anyone who desires to receive Christ in Eucharistic Communion must be in the state of grace. Anyone aware of having sinned mortally must not receive Communion without having received absolution in the sacrament of penance" (No. 1415). This is hardly new teaching.

Perhaps Catholics are no longer aware of what mortal sin is. The catechism again: "For a sin to be mortal, three conditions must together be met: Mortal sin is sin whose object is grave matter and which is also committed with full knowledge and deliberate consent" (No. 1857). Again, the same thing the Church has always taught.

Unfortunately, many Catholics seem to have rejected the whole concept of what comprises grave matter and therefore is mortal sin. The Church still teaches that all sexual activity (not just homosexual acts) outside of marriage is gravely sinful. So is deliberately missing Mass on weekends. The *Catechism of the Catholic Church* teaches that "those who deliberately fail in this obligation (to participate in the Eucharist on days of obligation) commit a grave sin" (No. 2181). People who do these things, without receiving absolution in the sacrament of penance, should know that they may not receive Communion.

CHAPTER 40

SOCIAL JUSTICE & CHARITY

Jesus left no doubt about how we are going to be judged at the end of the world. The twenty-fifth chapter of Matthew's Gospel, verses 31-46, tell us plainly that we will be saved if we feed the hungry, give drink to the thirsty, welcome the stranger, clothe the naked, and visit the sick and those in prison. Conversely, those who do not do that will be condemned.

The Catholic Church as an institution does all those things. Every diocese spends considerable resources on Catholic Charities or Catholic Social Services that help the poor, the immigrants, the homeless, and others in need. Catholic hospitals care for the sick and Catholic chaplains are assigned to other hospitals. The Saint Vincent de Paul Society aids the hungry and those who need clothing or household appliances. There is also a ministry to those in prison.

The Church's services aren't confined only to this country either. Catholic Relief Services, an agency of the Catholic bishops, is not only a relief agency in poor countries throughout the world, but it especially helps the poor in those countries learn to help themselves. By any standard you can think of, most people in the Western world enjoy a better standard of living than those in so-called developing nations. It's our obligation, therefore, to help those people to the best of our ability.

The Church's social doctrine flows from its belief that the human person is sacred. Each individual not only has the right to life but to all those things that are required for human decency. The *Catechism of the Catholic Church* says, "The decisive point of the social question is that goods created by God for everyone should in fact reach everyone in accordance with justice and with the help of charity" (No. 2459).

Meeting the needs of the poor, the sick, the homeless, immigrants, etc., is both a matter of justice and charity. In justice, we must try to remove the symptoms and causes of poverty and injustice. In charity, we must help those who are suffering from poverty and injustice.

This does not mean that inequality in society is always wrong, just when it becomes excessive. We don't all have the same talents and we don't all work as hard. It would be unjust, in fact, to reward everyone the same. The Church does not believe in socialism. In fact, it strongly condemns it.

The Church's social justice doctrine has been developed most thoroughly since 1891, when Pope Leo XIII wrote an encyclical titled *Rerum Novarum (On the Social Question)*. Since that time most of his successors have written their own encyclicals on that subject and the Second Vatican Council included social justice in its document *Gaudium et Spes (The Church in the Modern World)*.

An important aspect of the Church's social doctrine is what is called "the preferential option for the poor." That means that it's our obligation to put the needs of the poor and the vulnerable first. Exactly how it is best to do that in specific situations, though, is usually a matter of judgment.

The Church also teaches subsidiarity. This means that problems should be addressed at the lowest possible level, with communities of a higher order not interfering with the interior life of a community of a lower order. If a city government can handle a problem, the state government should not do so. If a state government can handle it, the country's government should not.

The *United States Catholic Catechism for Adults* tells us that "social justice is both an attitude and a practical response based on the principle that everyone should look at another person as another self. It is also a virtue that directs all the other virtues of individuals toward the common good" (Pg. 326).

CHAPTER 41

SEXUAL MORALITY

Sex is good. God created it and he created it good. He created men and women physically different so that they could unite in sexual activity and become two in one flesh. Furthermore, he created us with extremely strong desires for sex to make sure that we would want to unite with one another. That's the method he planned for us to co-create the human race.

However, he made us different from the animals, who also engage in sexual intercourse in order to reproduce. For humans, sexual intercourse is meant to be an act of love, an act of self-giving and receiving, an act that can be engaged in even when the woman is not fertile, an act that is licit only in a marriage between a man and a woman.

Modern society has rejected that idea. It probably began with the so-called "sexual revolution" in the 1960s, powered by the invention of the birth-control pill that made it possible for women to have sex with less fear of becoming pregnant. Then, as women became more sexually aggressive, men saw no reason to get married if their partner was willing to have sex with them without marriage. The ages at which men and women married gradually increased.

What happened to morality when all this was going on? When did it suddenly become all right for non-married men and women to have sex? Today our society takes it for granted that sexual activity is part of dating. Our television situation comedies revolve around men and women having sex outside of marriage.

The Catholic Church, therefore, is counter-cultural when it comes to sexual morality. It still teaches the virtue of chastity, which the *Catechism of the Catholic Church* defines as "the successful integration of sexuality within the person and thus the inner unity of man in his bodily and spiritual being" (No. 2337). Sexuality is more than just a physical act. Rather, it affects the whole person because of the unity of body and soul. We achieve chastity only through self-discipline, which can be a lifetime struggle because the sexual drive is powerful indeed.

Chastity is one of the vows that men and women Religious take, along with poverty and obedience. The virtue, though, is one that must be practiced by everyone, single and married. For the single it means no sexual activity of any kind—which, admittedly, is very difficult. For the married, it means sexual activity only with your spouse.

It's true that the Sixth Commandment says only, "You shall not commit adultery." Young single people have said to me, "I'm not committing adultery when I have sex with another single person." We believe, though, that this commandment forbids all sexual misbehavior. It is worded as it is to emphasize that sexual activity belongs in marriage and not outside it. Among the sins forbidden by this commandment are masturbation, fornication, pornography, and homosexual acts.

Contrary to those TV situation comedies, sexual activity between unmarried persons is sinful. It's called fornication, which might seem an old-fashioned word, but it's an action that's a lie in itself because it's an action that is meant for those in the committed bond of marriage.

Homosexuality is not wrong in itself and people with homosexual inclinations are not immoral. They must not be discriminated against. However, homosexual *acts* are immoral. The Church calls them "intrinsically disordered" because "they close the sexual act to the gift of life. They do not proceed from a genuine affective and sexual complementarity" (Catechism, No. 2357).

Married people must not only be faithful to one another, they must also permit every act of sexual intercourse to be open to the possibility of conceiving a child. The practice of natural family planning is a legitimate way for couples to avoid or achieve a pregnancy because it doesn't involve artificial contraception.

Both the unitive and procreative aspects of sexual activity are important, and they can be achieved only in marriage.

CHAPTER 42

DEVOTIONS AND SACRAMENTALS

Many people through the centuries have been attracted to the Catholic Church because of its many devotions. Catholics always seem to be doing something special, whether it's getting ashes put on their foreheads on Ash Wednesday, using incense at Mass, or blessing themselves with holy water. Some Protestants do some of the same things, depending on the denomination, but not as much as Catholics.

Some of those devotions are known as sacramentals. Like the sacraments, they are sacred signs, but they differ from the sacraments in that they were instituted by the Church rather than by Jesus. (There are a couple other technical differences, too.) Sacramentals include blessings, ceremonies such as processions, prayers such as the Divine Praises or the rosary, and various objects that are used for religious purposes such as candles, medals, or palms.

First among the sacramentals are blessings. Catholics have blessings for everything, or everyone—for sacred vessels used at Mass, for rosaries and medals, for leaders of congregations, for mothers and fathers, and the list could go on. A popular blessing is the blessing of throats on Saint Blaise's feast day because of the legend that that otherwise obscure martyr once cured a boy who had gotten a fishbone caught in his throat. (Catholics do seem to like to receive things at Mass—Saint Blaise's blessing, ashes on Ash Wednesday, and palms on Palm Sunday, for example.)

Catholics, of course, also bless themselves when they make the Sign of the Cross while invoking the Blessed Trinity—Father, Son and Holy Spirit. When entering or leaving a Catholic church, they bless themselves with holy water from a font by the entrance, and holy water is also used in the blessing of other objects. Parents teach their children from an early age to bless themselves with the Sign of the Cross. We also ask for God's blessing when we say grace before meals.

Processions don't seem to be as popular among Catholics in the United States as they are in other countries, but they still exist in our churches—especially on the feast of Corpus Christi or on Holy Thursday when consecrated hosts are moved from the altar to a tabernacle elsewhere in the church to be used on Good Friday. In many countries, especially in Italy and Latin American countries, processions through the streets of the city on a saint's feast day are quite popular.

Since all of us are different in the things we like to do, there are Catholic devotions or forms of piety to match any preferences. Our churches have the Stations of the Cross on the side walls for people who like to make the Way of the Cross on Fridays or during Lent. These are fourteen depictions of Jesus' march to Calvary, from his condemnation to death through his burial. Other Catholics like to light candles by side altars dedicated to the Blessed Virgin or saints. We're all familiar with photos of the many candles lit at the Grotto at the University of Notre Dame. The Grotto is a replica of the place where Mary appeared to Saint Bernadette in Lourdes, France.

Pilgrimages remain extremely popular, especially to the Holy Land, Rome, Assisi, or to some of the Marian shrines—Lourdes, Fatima, Lujan, Czestochowa, or the Shrine of the Immaculate Conception in Washington. Some Catholics like to make novenas, which are special prayers said for a period of nine days, usually in petition for special favors. Others have special devotion to the Sacred Heart of Jesus, the Divine Mercy of Jesus, or to saints such as Francis or Therese. Many Catholics wear crosses, medals or scapulars (pieces of cloth with pictures of a saint) around their necks.

The bells in our churches ring three times a day to remind Catholics to say the *Angelus*, so-named because it begins, "The angel of the Lord." The prayer reminds us of the Incarnation—that the angel appeared to Mary, who agreed to become the mother of God, and then the Word was made flesh and dwelt among us.

The number of special Catholic devotions seems endless. There's something there for every taste. They are powerful forms of prayer that have proved to be of spiritual benefit down through the centuries.

CPSIA information can be obtained at www.ICGtesting.com
Printed in the USA
LVOW06s1108130813

347664LV00001B/45/P